Relationship Reminders

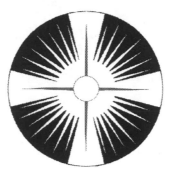

Practical Guidance
for
Conscious Relating

Betty Lue Lieber, PhD, MFT

BALBOA.
PRESS

A DIVISION OF HAY HOUSE

ISBN: 978-1-4525-5202-6 (sc)
ISBN: 978-1-4525-5203-3 (e)

Balboa Press books may be ordered through booksellers or by contacting:

Balboa Press
A Division of Hay House
1663 Liberty Drive
Bloomington, IN 47403
www.balboapress.com
1-(877) 407-4847

Because of the dynamic nature of the Internet, any web addresses or links contained in this book may have changed since publication and may no longer be valid. The views expressed in this work are solely those of the author and do not necessarily reflect the views of the publisher, and the publisher hereby disclaims any responsibility for them.

The author of this book does not dispense medical advice or prescribe the use of any technique as a form of treatment for physical, emotional, or medical problems without the advice of a physician, either directly or indirectly. The intent of the author is only to offer information of a general nature to help you in your quest for emotional and spiritual well-being. In the event you use any of the information in this book for yourself, which is your constitutional right, the author and the publisher assume no responsibility for your actions.

Printed in the United States of America

Balboa Press rev. date: 7/24/2012

Other books by Betty Lue Lieber, PhD, MFT

Loving Reminders 2000

Peaceful Reminders 2001

Relationship Reminders 2003, 2012

Healing Reminders 2012

Healthy Reminders 2012

Family Reminders 2012

May your relationships be blessed with
healing, appreciation, creativity and joy.

May you remember always the Love You Are.

Betty Lue

Contents

Preface

*Loving Reminders are written **for me and for you.** Usually early in the morning, I sit and write whatever comes to me. There is no hesitancy or forethought, but rather a spontaneous pouring forth of whatever I am called to write. For a gift to be fully given spiritually, it must be fully received by the messenger. I receive it for myself and rarely correct typos.*

Everything is perceived through the filters of the recipient. I trust you will interpret what you read through your own filters and beliefs, judgments and life experience. Together we are exploring our world and the integration of spiritual principles in everyday life.

I am with you because I am You. You each represent a part of me that seeks to love and be loved. You show up in my life as teacher and learner, so I can learn what I am teaching and see in you what I have learned. The mirror can be directed in many ways for me to see mySelf, my Whole Self, in all its many facets, personalities, bodies and missions. Betty Lue

Acknowledgments

Loving Reminders flow from my quiet Mind and Open Heart, where I listen to the Voice Within, the Holy Spirit, that lives within each one of us.

Thank you Spirit.

You, the readers, have been my inspiration, my reason, and my encouragement for putting reminders into book form.

Thank you Friends.

My Life Partner, Robert Waldon, is my helpmate and support in bringing the printed form to you with spiritual integrity. Thank you Robert.

I am forever grateful to the Love that lives within me and sets me free to totally trust in the Love We Are together.

Thank you Love.

Introduction

Our Relationship

As you open this book and begin to read, **you are beginning a relationship with me, the writer,** with the spiritual energy that works through me, with the words contained herein and most importantly with Love ItSelf. In this physical world we see ourselves as separate, yet we can be in relationship with all things in order to better know our whole Selves, the One.

Be aware that this book is not perfect in the worldly, comparative sense. You will find mistakes within these pages. The same is true of your relationship with me and with yourself. You and I will make mistakes within our time together. Such is the nature of physical life. To the degree you focus on the errors, they will seemingly grow and take over your field of vision. However, if you can forgive your judgments and see beyond the errors to the Essence or Heart of this book and the reminders it offers, you will be healed of the pain, frustration, loneliness and depression you may have felt.

Forgive me and you will know me. Forgive mistakes and you will receive the blessing. Release comparison and you will experience only the Goodness and come to know the Love You Are and how to share Your Whole Self more fully and freely with others.

My Teacher

Holy Spirit or the *Voice Within* has guided me faithfully, answering every question and responding to every request. I feel always loved, supported and provided for in every need. I need do nothing, except remember **I am here to give freely the Highest I know to those who are sent.**

I recognize that teachers and students are simply those at different levels of awareness for a temporary period of time. The teacher gives a hand to the student to lift them to a higher perspective. The student is called to the teacher who is able to provide the next opportunity to awaken. As the student and teacher fully open and appreciate their teaching-learning relationship, Spirit enters in and provides all that is needed for both.

I teach as I learn. I give as I receive. Along the path, the Spiritual Seeker seeks outside themselves what is already within, quietly waiting to be discovered. Periodically I am called to simplify and return to the basics. I release everything that does not support me in being the Love and Light I Am.

Our function here is forgiveness, releasing everything that is not Love. We are here to set ourselves free to be the LOVE WE ARE. Seeking for nothing, simply being what we already are and have always been: LOVE.

About My Process

I am writing these remainders for you and for myself. We are in a relationship that I value and want to enhance. We are friends and partners on the spiritual path, seeking to be more and give more of the Love We Are. Not everyone is aware of this path. So we model for them bringing the Light and the Love inside by extending it to everyone.

I am obvious. My words speak for me. My heart and mind are an open book. You see me and know me and love me through these words. More importantly, you come to know I truly love and care for you. I am responsible for the wholeness and holiness in our relationship. I give to you the best I know. All I have is given to you with no conditions. These words are free to everyone. These books can be shared with anyone who would receive them as gift. They are here to be truly helpful. If there is anything that does not resonate or feel right or true to you, let it go. Waste no energy on resisting, arguing or avoiding, simply let go and move on in your own "right" direction. You know your own sacred journey and it is yours to honor, just as I respect and honor my own.

Relationship Blessing

Bless those who Love.
    May they know the Love of God.
Bless those who forget.
    May they remember the Love They Are.
Bless those who forgive.
    May they realize their sinlessness.
Bless those who condemn.
    May they recognize they are forgiven.
Bless those who appreciate.
    May they enjoy the fullness of life.
Bless those who find fault.
    May they realize their own perfection.
Bless those who are true friends.
    May they reach out with faith and gratitude.
Bless those who are lonely.
    May they receive the comfort they need.
Bless those who are bountiful.
    May they share their abundance with joy.
Bless those who are needy.
    May they share what they have and prosper.
Bless those who know God.
    May they live in Peace.
Bless those who seek God.
    May they find the Good within.

Loving

Love Your Self

To experience Love in our relationships, we must experience Love within ourselves.

To receive the Love we give, we must remember to give this Love to ourselves.

Where we feel neglected, disrespected, unseen, unsupported and unloved, we must first to heal our relationship with ourselves.

Clear your unconscious programming with these affirmations. Say, write and meditate on them daily.

Stop when you truly experience Love for yourself.

Change the exact words to apply specifically to you.

I forgive myself for putting others first.
I forgive myself for neglecting my own needs.
I now give myself what is Best for me.
What is best for me benefits others.
I love, trust and respect myself.
Love works through my thoughts, words and deeds.
I am healed, whole and holy.
I am willing to listen and follow the Voice Within.
All things work together for Good.
I learn from everyone as everyone learns from me.
I am blessed, as I bless everyone, including myself.
I am created by Love to express Love and live in Love.

Love Is Our Work

Unconditional Love heals, creates, nourishes and sustains life.

How do we grow unconditional Love in us?

When we forget, ignore, withhold or diminish Love, we feel guilty and seek to judge and blame. When others forget, ignore, withhold or diminish Love, we may feel hurt, angry, defensive or devalued.

In either case, whether we forget or they forget, we must forgive immediately. We must demonstrate with our thoughts and prayers, our words and affirmation, our deeds and acts of kindness that we remember to Love Unconditionally.

Our work is to remember Love.
Our work is to extend Love.
Our work is to exalt Love.
Our work is to live in Love.

Encourage Love in your mind and heart.
Appreciate Love both in yourself and in others.
Give Love freely to everyone at all times.
Let your Love Light shine with Joy and Gratitude.

This is our true vocation: to return to our Natural State—Unconditional Love.

Real Love

What is Love? Real Love.
Only Love is real, everything else illusion.
Love heals .... Fear hurts.
Love succeeds... Fear fails.
Love persists .... Fear quits.
Love answers .... Fear asks.
Love fulfills.. Fear depletes.
Love needs nothing.................................... Fear needs everything.
Love is patient .... Fear is impatient.
Love believes .... Fear doubts.
Love trusts... Fear suspects.
Love frees... Fear limits.
Love unites .... Fear divides.
Love is willing... Fear is demanding.
Love accepts .... Fear judges.
Love forgives .... Fear condemns.

What is fear?
Fear is the absence of Love.
Fear is the call for love.
Fear is the experience of separation from Love.

What is Love?
Love is all that is real and lasting, changeless and eternal.
Love is All.

Important Gifts of Love

What is most important to give to those we love?

Trust   Trust in their process of learning.
Respect   Treat them as we would want.
Freedom   Give them space to explore.
Patience   Give them time to learn.
Openness   Listen to their true feelings.
Forgiveness Easily release their mistakes.
Support   Believe in their dreams.
Truth   Be honest and open in your truth.
Kindness   Be gentle in how you speak.
Gratitude   Appreciate their Goodness.

Everyone is a Spiritual Being having a human existence with their unique history, memories, hopes and fears, strengths and areas of needed learning.

Everyone deserves to live and love, learn and laugh, let go and begin again.

You are the One who gives yourself these opportunities first.

When you are loving you, you can love everyone equally with the Highest gifts of love you know.

As you love others fully and freely, both you and they will heal and be blessed with boundless Love..

Loving Is A Way of Life

Loving is a way of life.
Loving is a spiritual discipline.
Loving is the way to peace and happiness.
Loving is our reason for being here.
Loving is the way home.
Loving is a committed connection to Spirit.
Loving is conscious thoughts, words and deeds.
Loving is a lifetime vocation.
Loving is a choice, the choice to be Real.
Loving is freeing yourself and trusting yourself.

****

When I am loving, I am grateful.
If I cannot be grateful, I forgive myself for forgetting.
When I am grateful, I experience more to be grateful for.
When I forget, I see false evidence of my ingratitude. Complaining is the lazy way to live.
Gratitude requires conscious commitment to Love.
Gratitude invites taking responsibility for limited perception.

I forgive myself for limiting my perception.
I forgive myself for forgetting to be grateful.
I forgive forgetting to bless everything with my Love.
I forgive my limited perceiving and bless my world.
As I forgive my limited perception, I am grateful.
I am willing to remember always and only to Love.

Love Is Freedom and Trust

♥ I love you ♥

and I know you love me, too.

LOVE IS FREEDOM

the freedom for you and I to be who we are,

the freedom to live life as we do,

the freedom to make mistakes and learn from them,

the freedom to express our own truth as we see it.

LOVE IS TRUST

the trust that there is a constant flow of love,

no matter what,

the trust that in spite of life's problems,

we believe in & support each other's right to live as we choose,

the trust that in adversity

there is healing and learning and gifts of love,

the trust that under conflict and emotional expression,

there is always love.

I love you and I trust you and

I free you to be all you are.

Freedom or Fear

One Gift of Love is Freedom.
We are all created in Love as Love for the purpose of Loving. In the denseness of this world, we may forget our Source, our Identity and our Purpose. We are created Free as Freedom-Givers for the purpose of Freeing others to be Free.
Freedom means making errors and experiencing consequences.
Freedom means we can explore many diverse paths.
Freedom means we are responsible.
Freedom means we are always at choice.
Freedom means we have infinite possibilities always before us. Freedom means we must choose our own unique path. Freedom means we choose.

Fear may show up to oppose Love and Freedom.
If we believe we are created in Fear as Fear-teachers for the purpose of limiting ourselves and others, we live in fear and distrust life. If we see ourselves as afraid, we avoid and resist freedom. If we teach fear, we limit others and keep them from being free.
If we "love" with fear, we hold others back by warning, care-taking, protecting and preventing them from experiencing freedom of choice and the consequences. If we are afraid of life, we will find ways to limit the freedom, abundance and magnificence in life for ourselves and others.
In fear, Love is not realized. In fear we can only react, defend and protect our own position, beliefs and territory.
When I know I am free, I know I am loved.
When I know I am loved, I know I am free.
I choose Love.
I choose to be free.
I free you to choose without questioning your choices.
I choose to honor the gift of freedom.
I choose to Love You.

Love Never Quits

Once you have loved, you will always love..... unless you allow fear and guilt, ego and self-forgetting to get in the way.

Love does not quit on anyone for any reason.

Fear, judgment, guilt, anger, and hurt hide our awareness of Love's Presence.

When we allow another's behavior or external situations to stop us from Loving, from being the gift of Love we really are, we have unconsciously chosen to let fear lead the way. Because we are here to love and be loved, we feel guilty for quitting on our soul purpose. We will project our guilt onto the other with blame. We will try to get the other out of our lives. We will seek to avoid those feelings of guilt for making ourselves unhappy. Choosing to give another the power to shut us down, choosing to be off purpose, choosing to hurt another, choosing to be angry or cruel hurts us more than we know.

It is important to realize that only we can correct our error. Only through complete forgiveness can we begin again.

We must see ourselves and this relationship in a new light.

We must begin again with a new attitude.

We must make a new commitment within ourselves.

The single most important decision I have ever made is:

I will never quit on Love.

I will never quit on mySelf.

I will never quit on being the Love I Am.

The only mistake we ever make is when we forget to Love.

I forgive myself for ever forgetting.

I choose to love everyone no matter what.

What decision are you willing to make?

Love is My Employer

Love is my Employer.
Spirit is my Boss.
Those I serve are my inspirational customers.
I honor the mission of my employer and direction of my boss.
I am given provision by those I serve that I might serve more.
My commission is the Joy I receive from giving my very Best.
I am serving Love, my Employer, every moment.
I honor my Boss, whenever I am serving Love.

All forms of provision, whether tithes or gifts, praise or payment, contribution or caring, are my salary to care for my human family's needs and my spiritual customers.

This is my business here in the world.
Who is your Employer? Who is your Boss?
Who do you listen to for direction each day?
Whom do you serve and How do you serve?
When you are giving your very Best, how do you feel?
Whether employed, self-employed or a life as a "volunteer" or minister of Good, you have a spiritual calling.

There are a spiritual employer and boss who are providing for you and applauding your Good works.

You have a purpose wherever you work.

Awareness

Relationships

Every relationship is for the purpose of healing.

Every relationship is a place to give and receive Love.

Every relationship is given to Spirit or to our ego.

Every relationship has a purpose.

There are no chance encounters.

When we are serving Love, we see Love in every One.

We give the Love we have to every One.

There is no one left outside our Love.

When we are serving our egoic needs, we see the flaws, the lacks, the woundedness in others. We withhold our love.

We look for what we get in return. Most special or needy relationships have both pleasure and pain. They "work", when we get what we want, and they "hurt" when we are not getting outcome we desire. These are conditional relationships. They resemble past experiences, until we realize we can change our response. This is our relationship response-ability.

Each of us has the opportunity to heal our past and heal expectations by responding differently. We can forgive our judgmental reactions and respond with love. Healing and transformation may take time, but often is immediate with miracles of Love.

The most important change is within our selves.

Drop expectations.

Become a Love giver instead of a fault finder.

Life works because we do the work.

Your consciousness and inner pictures create your relationships as you experience them. You can change the inner pictures and perceptions you no longer want.

You can be conscious and forgive the unconscious past similars that keep coming up.

You can be the conscious one!

Just keep on loving, no matter what.

Challenging Relationships

There are no accidents in the relationships we attract.

When there are challenges or difficulties in relating, we must remember that there is valuable learning and healing potential in every relationship.

Challenging relationships offer lessons in patience, acceptance, forgiveness and trust. They teach us how to be strong in our commitment to love no matter what. Within them we can strengthen our willingness to love as God loves, without condition and never quitting on Love.

People with whom we have difficulty often represent a part of ourselves. They may be ourselves as we used to be in the recent or distant past—hurting, sensitive, depressed, angry, fearful, unaware. Or they may be parts of our personality that we judge and try not to admit.

We are healing our tendency to criticize, blame, fear, resist, ignore, withhold love and allow others to upset us.

With ourselves and others we are learning to offer comfort, reassurance, loving reminders, a helping hand, forgiveness and unconditional Love.

All relationships are to help us heal our past.

Every relationship is a lesson in Love.

We are here to remember Love and return to Wholeness.

Focus Creates

What we see in others, we strengthen in ourselves.
To focus on neediness, we become more needy.
To judge greediness, we become more greedy.
To focus on disease, we may become sick.
To attend to the wounded, we can feel their hurt.
Blessing a Holy One, we are blessed with our own Holiness.
Igniting the Light in a brother, our own Light shines brighter.
Reminding One who has forgotten reminds us as well.
To make another happy, heals and makes us happy and whole.

What are you paying attention to right now?
How do you choose to focus your activities?
What invites your thinking and feeling?
What is inspiring you and calling to you?
Distraction, urgency or release?
What has happened, what may happen or what is happening now?
Are you regretting, anticipating or experiencing?
Life is just choices.
Each choice helps you notice what you value and what you want.
Contentment and peace come from valuing what you want with all your thoughts, words and your choice of activities.

Projections

Everything is a projection from our own experience.
If I am clever, I expect and project others are, too.
If I am secretive, I imagine the same for you.
If I am manipulative or controlling, I will see this in you.
Where I see myself and my life, I will imagine the same for you.
unless……..
I make no assumptions.
I see things as they really are.
I look for the inner Truth.
I choose to know nothing and learn everything.
I listen to you and honor your heart.

I cannot know what your intention is unless I ask.
I must clarify everything with you.
I can offer feedback about what I think I hear, and then ask, "Is this true?"

In relationships, we have roles and functions in others' lives.
Our words are given meaning that is not our intention.
Our presence brings up feelings and thoughts in others which we cannot even imagine.
We are all actors on one another's stage, playing parts imagined through the historical patterns and images of our own inner world.
Remember to look for the inner Truth.

Choose what you want to see.

Choose Responsibly

One of the keys to a successful relationship is the willingness to take total responsibility without guilt or blame for the quality of that relationship.

Where there is fear, I cannot love.
Where there is phoniness, I cannot trust.
Where there is blame, I cannot resolve.
Where there is denial, I cannot understand.

I am responsible for what I see.
I am responsible for what I hear.
I am responsible for how I feel.
I am responsible for how I respond.

The choice is mine.
I choose what I believe.
I choose what I think and do.
I choose what to celebrate and to judge.
I choose how I live.

Our choices are powerful.
Our choices are messages we give our world.
Our choices teach Love or fear.
Our choices teach Peace or violence.
Our choices teach Forgiveness or vengeance.
Our choices teach Happiness or suffering.
Our choices teach Helpfulness or ignorance.

Co-Dependence and Inter-Dependence

Functional community and families are interdependent. *Everyone knows their function and role and fulfills their part for the good of the whole.*

What interferes with fully functioning families and communities is the readiness and willingness of the members to function in an interdependent manner. Each one recognizes their part is integral to the whole and is willing to give their best to fulfill their function. When there is a belief that one part is not as important or some individuals give half-heartedly, the result is limited in some way.

In a fully functioning relationship or community, participants must be self-actualized, having fulfilled their own personal achievements, they are free to give to a co-creative whole. What works best is conscious authentic beings who genuinely want to contribute to the good of the whole.

Stages of relationship development include:

Dependence, Independence and Interdependence.

To be fully functioning we need to complete each level in ourselves. When another genuinely needs to be dependent, we step out of our independence and respond with support. When we need to partner to complete a project or help our family, we work interdependently which invites everyone to participate giving their best for the success of the whole.

Look at your own development.

See where you are.

Look for areas of resistance or ignorance.

What you can do to live and teach the value of all three.

I am dependent on God.

I am free and independent in my life choices.

I am interdependent for the good of the whole.

Everything I think, say and do teaches and affects everyone.

False Assumptions About Relationships

"Other people are just like me."
"If other people are not like me, they should be."
"My view of the world is accurate."
"I know how to have a relationship."
"If we really love each other, it should be easy."

People are different in the ways they think, speak and behave. We all are creatures of our history, habits and beliefs.

When we acknowledge and appreciate our differences, there is much to learn and teach, give and receive, with one another to expand our awareness and our repertoire of behaviors.

If everyone were like us, we would have nothing to learn, nothing to heal, and nothing to balance our lives.

Everyone is totally unique in what they have to learn and teach. Everyone comes with their own message and gifts to give.

Our differences enrich our lives beyond measure.

Our beliefs, opinions and judgments color our perceptions.

We all see something different from one another.

What we believe we see and filter out what we don't believe.

We cannot trust our instincts about relationships, because they are based on faulty information, limited possibilities and fearful or defensive attitudes. When we open to include new information, other's perceptions and novel possibilities, we are open to benefits for all. Use inner guidance as your frame of reference, seeing and believing in the highest good for all concerned.

When we commit to Love someone, we have begun the journey to do the work to undo all the prejudices, fears and past failures. When we commit to Love, we have begun to correct our misperceptions, to forgive our judgments, to let go of our past history and to create from within a new way of relating. We have begun to recognize and release all the blocks we have set in place to hide our awareness of the Presence of Love in every one.

Conscious Loving Is Remembering

Conscious Remembering is experienced when we:
1. Dedicate the relationship to the Highest Good.
2. Set a conscious goal or desired outcome.
3. Honor our whole and Holy Self in each moment.
4. Remember Who We Are and the purpose for relating.

When conscious:

We remember Love and Happiness are our natural state.

We remember we are a Loving Reminder.

We remember Love is the purpose for our Being.

We remember all relationships are for healing the past.

We remember Love is for "giving", not for "getting".

We realize life is meaningless without freedom and trust

We remember we are here to teach what we are learning.

We remember everything we think, say and do is teaching.

We remember that knowing, loving and respecting ourselves teaches others how to know, love and respect all.

We remember that all forgiveness is really a gift to ourselves.

We remember that every relationship is a lesson in Love.

We remember as we heal ourselves, we are healing others.

We remember giving forgiveness and gratitude are the fastest way to heal.

We remember it is up to the most conscious person to extend forgiveness and love.

We remember that successful relationships entail sharing a common goal, expressing the High Truth, giving and receiving the Best, committing to what is truly best for all and taking full responsibility for the quality of the relationship without guilt and blame.

We remember conscious loving means we do not hurt another nor allow another to hurt us.

We remember to never quit on loving.

Conscious relationships are a path to enlightenment and mastery.

Keys To Successful Relationships

Seek a common vision or goal for both parties.
True happiness, a healthy family, serving humanity are all good goals.

Communicate honestly what you want both to have.
When you want peace and happiness for both, say it.
When you are having difficulty and want help, say it.
No secrets, no mystery, no assumptions or withholds, no gossiping about relationship issues. Respect the other and value your relationships.

Be willing to give positive energy and regard.
Be willing to give and receive, teach and learn, talk and listen. Relationships that are one-sided will fail to thrive and succeed. There must be equality and reciprocity. There must be a willingness to contribute your fair share for the good of all.

Commit to what is best for both.
Commit to the highest good for all parties. Don't hold back or control the other. Free yourself and give freedom to the other to live their dreams. Don't demand or threaten. Request and respect their answer. Threats to quit any relationship always undermine the fabric of security With threat of leaving, there is no safety and no respect for the value of the relationship

Respond with love to the needs of the relationship.
To take full responsibility for the quality of a relationship one must be conscious and fulfilled. When either party is needy, their dependency distorts the responsibility of both parties. When either party is perceived as holding more power, there is fear. It is essential that each person be in the relationship feel free and trusting.. When we believe there are no options we feel trapped or restricted. Take full responsibility for the quality of the relationship without guilt or blame.

Joining, Honesty, Equality, Commitment and Responsibility are Keys to Successful Relationships.

Wake Up

Whenever I am conflicted or unhappy, I have a wakeup call.
All wakeups are a call to stop, look and listen within.
A lack of peace tells me I am off purpose, not living in integrity or not being true to my self.
Every upset is a wakeup call.

<u>Messages:</u>
Wake up and listen within.
Wake up and speak up.
Wake up and heal the past.
Wake up and forgive yourself
Wake up and choose again.
Wake up and honor your Self.
Wake up and clean up your life.

If I keep remembering some incident or relationship, it means I am not complete with my part.
Where I am not living in present moment, I am incomplete with my past.

The call is to return to the unconscious omission or commission. Ask, *"What am I to do to complete this?"*
When I am complete, I am at peace.
When I am at peace, I have given my best.
When I have given my best, I have played my part.
When I have played my part, I can rest.

Let's Wake Up Smiling

Be Aware:
See what we have chosen, our learning, our perceptions, our judgments and fears, our illusions of limitation and lack.

Be Acknowledging:
Express what we want to see differently, where we want healing and transformation of our perceptions.

Be Allowing:
Let go of our mistakes and faulty thinking.
Release the illusion and forgive ourselves.

Be Open:
Sit in silence in the void and listen to what is calling for you.

Be Affirming:
State clearly the choice to know only Truth, see only Light, and experience wholeness and goodness and beauty. Choose for the Highest and Best for such is God's Will.

Be Accepting:
All Good is our Divine Right, so honor and respect and receive the Good you truly deserve.

Be Appreciative:
Give joyful thanks for all Good and be generous in your gifts to the Source of all Good.

To awaken is to forgive the world and heal the past.

Enlightenment is seeing what is good, beautiful and holy.

We Are All Teachers

We are teaching all with our thoughts.
What we believe, what we pay attention to, what we judge, what we care about, what we fear, all are teaching our world telepathically, because our minds are connected. Thoughts are things. Our thoughts create, either blessing or cursing, creating or destroying, helping or hurting, honoring or disrespecting.
May we think thoughts which teach our world what we want our world to be.
We are teaching with our words.
The words we write and speak and the words we read and listen to teach others. For as we fill our minds and other minds with notions of possibility or impossibility, hope or despair, love or fear, peace or anger, we are encouraging and leading our circle of influence and beyond to follow our chosen path.
May we offer words of kindness and wisdom leading others to kindness and wisdom.
We are teaching with our example.
Our lifestyle and daily activities, done in secret or in public, are a powerful testimony of what we believe and hold in high regard. We are not only measured by our example, but are believed and followed by those who admire us and look to us to lead and to learn from.
May we live valuing what is for the Good of all, teaching the world a better way.
Teaching our world, our community, our families is a natural by product of our everyday life. We do make a difference.
May we recognize, respect and appreciate ourselves for choosing the extraordinary path rather than what is common. May we lead and teach consciously and wisely with our thoughts, words and activities.

You Are Called

What does it take to be fully present?
What does it take to be in Love with All?
What does it take to do no harm?
What does it take to be truly helpful?
What does it take to never be upset and hurt?
What does it take to be perfectly happy?

You are called to be conscious.
You are called to take responsibility.
You are called to be totally respectful.
You are called to listen within.
You are called to forgive all the time.
You are called to claim your Holiness.
You are called to see only wholeness.
You are called to seek the Highest Good.
You are called to choose win/win solutions.
You are called to take impeccable self-care.
You are called to be peaceful and happy.
You are called to live what you teach.
You are called to love all equally.
You are called be totally honest.
You are called to be authentic.
You are called to appreciate the gift in everything.
You are called to be All You Are.

Self Love

Flower Poem

If you would grow to your best self
Be patient, not demanding,
Accepting, not condemning,
Nurturing, not withholding,
Self-marveling, not belittling,
Gently guiding, not pushing & punishing.

For you are more sensitive than you know.
Mankind is tough as war,
Yet delicate as flowers.
We can endure agonies,
But we open fully only to warmth & light.

And our need to grow
Is fragile as a fragrance
Dispersed by storms of will
To return only when those storms are still.

So accept, respect,
Attend your sensitivity.
A flower cannot be opened with a hammer.

Love Created You

Love created You like ItSelf.
Love created you Loving.
Peace created you Peaceful.
Joy created you Joyous.
Holiness created You Holy.

When we are not wholly loving, peaceful and joyous, we have made a mistake.
We have stepped away from the Truth of Who We Are.
We have allowed the world of apparency to mislead us.
We have allowed fear to be our teacher.
We have chosen a false and faulty path.
This world has many temptations to seduce us.
There are many distractions to call our attention.
There are alternative paths and plans to detour us.
There are many excuses to delay our conscious choice.

If we want the Love we seek…
If we want to live in Joy…..
If we want to be at Peace…,
We must choose the path of Holiness.

Choose the most loving response to all things.

What You See Lies Within You

What you see in others, lives somewhere in you.
It may be a past memory of being what you see.
It may be an ideal quality which you hold.
It may be a fear you have learned.

If you can see it somewhere in your being, you must first know it and believe it. Everything we see is not True, but rather is the interpretation, the projection of our own belief on the mirror of the outer world or a reflection of what is held in our inner world.

To love yourself unconditionally is to open the door to love others without judgment.
If you learn to be wholly forgiving of your own mistakes, it becomes easy and natural to forgive others their mistakes.

Each of us is responsible for clearing our own mind, for choosing to forgive and clean away the false thinking and illusions of the past.
We must allow the Vision of the Wholeness, Goodness and Beauty to fully enter our minds and be fully embraced by our consciousness in order to live the Love We Are.

I believe in Good, therefore I see the Good.
I believe in Love, therefore I see the Love.
I believe in Peace, therefore I see the Peace.

Believe in the Peace and Love and Good in You.

Loving Yourself

You are teaching your world how to perceive you and treat you by how you see and treat yourself.

You are also teaching your world by how you perceive and treat others.

When you love, trust and respect yourself, you will love, trust and respect others.

When you doubt your worthiness, you will doubt others' worthiness.

When you treat yourself with neglect or cruelty in thought, word or action, you may teach others this is what you deserve and desire.

<u>Affirmations:</u>
The more I love, trust and respect myself,
the more I love, trust and respect others.

The more I love, trust and respect myself,
the more others love, trust and respect me.

The more I love, trust and respect myself,
the more others love, trust and respect themselves.

The more I love, trust and respect myself, the more others love, trust and respect others.

How can I love, trust and respect myself more?
Make a commitment to demonstrate your choice for more self love and self respect daily.

Loyalty

Are you loyal to yourself?
Some of us are loyal to others.
Some of us are loyal to our beliefs.
Some of us are loyal to groups.
Some of us are loyal to causes.

If we forsake ourselves to follow another, we are living out of integrity.
If we abandon ourselves to be with another, we are denying ourselves.
If we listen to others and not ourselves, we are teaching self-forgetting.
If we value loyalty, it must be our choice to be loyal to ourselves first and foremost.

When I am loyal to my wholeness, I am healthy.
When I am loyal to my values, I model integrity.
When I am loyal to my mission, I strengthen my life purpose.
When I am loyal to my Essence, I am happy and free.

Be loyal to your Authentic Self.

First Things First

The voices of the world call to us from every corner of our lives. Our "shoulds", "have-tos", needs and desires call for our attention. The demands of health, finance, family, job and home all call to us.

How do we respond?
What are our priorities?
When do we say "No"?
When is there open time, quiet time, inner time, peaceful time?

When I know my goal is inner peace, I choose to listen.
My function is to lay aside the distractions, detours and delays.
My function is to forgive, erase and release my fears.
My function is to listen within to the Voice for Good, the still small inner voice within. I set aside time to listen within to the guidance that calls me home to my Higher Self., the Essence of Me.
When I am quiet, undistracted and unattached to having control over the outcome I have made up, I am willing to be led by the guidance of Spirit and listen for what inspires me and offers peace.
In this I find wisdom, peace, comfort, assurance and direction in which no one loses.
In this, I am happy and at peace.

<u>**Listen within as you ask:**</u>
Where am I to go?
What am I to do?
What am I to say and to whom?

Living In Integrity

What sets us free is living in integrity.
With nothing to hide
And nothing to fear,
We are free to live.
Our life is clear.

What is integrity?
Integrity is having the courage to live what you believe.
Integrity is having the courage to speak your heartfelt Truth.
Integrity is having the courage to give what is really your Best.
Integrity is having the courage to think only what serves all.
Integrity is the courage to make your world a better place.
Integrity is living everyday as you want your world to see.
Integrity is having nothing to hide and totally free.

I invite you to look today to any behavior, habit, thought or relationship
about which you are ashamed, fearful or secretive. Let it go.
If it is not the Best you know, it is not worthy of You.
You will feel worthy of Love, respect and a life of abundance when
you are the Good you know.
Create your whole life well and you will be free.
Create your whole life beautiful and you will be free.
Create your whole life Good and you will be free.

Joy In Union

It is in Union that all things are manifest.
Wherever two or more are joined in Love, all things are possible.
The world is made up by agreement.

It is in the present moment that we find our Inner Joy.
It is in our Joy that we are fully living in the moment.

So much time, energy and money is spent on finding and avoiding what is not our joy.

So many resources are expended on seeking a future of happiness.

Avoiding the pain and seeking the pleasure distract us from being fully present right now.

The past and the future divert our precious Presence and the Joy that comes from being fully here now.

Know yourself by finding your Joy.
Love yourself by choosing your Joy.
Support yourself by committing to your Joy.

It is in Joy that you lose your false self and find your True Self.
It is in Union with your whole Self that miracles happen.

Come into relationship with your Whole Self.
Reunite with the One you are and Joy is yours.

True Support

Those with whom you associate become your support team.
Their reflection is the mirror through which you see yourself.

Where you are loved, you see yourself as loveable.
Where you are trusted, you see yourself as trustworthy.
Where you are appreciated, you see yourself as valuable.
Where you are admired, you see yourself as admirable.

Teach the people around you that you are loveable.
Be loving to all.
Teach your friends you are trustworthy.
Trust your friends.
Be consistent in your speech and behavior.
Live in integrity in thought, word and deed.
Teach your associates you are valuable.
Value everyone equally.

Show yourself by being the happy and bountiful gift you are.
Give freely of your gratitude and natural joy.
Your beauty and goodness and worth have nothing to do with external things given or taught.
Your worth is intrinsic, natural and essential within you.

Shine your Light.
Live in Love.
Walk in Beauty.
Express your Joy.

All will see and reflect your Goodness and Wholeness and Beauty right back to you.

Twelve Daily Steps To Optimistic Living

* Focus on successes rather than on failures.
* Notice what is accomplished rather than left undone.
* See beauty rather than imperfections.
* Notice choosing optimum conditions, rather than judging times of mistaken choices.
* Acknowledge all wins each and every day.
* Create and maintain an environment that nurtures.
* See problems as opportunities to learn, rather than as obstacles to avoid.
* Tell the whole truth on a moment to moment basis in order to maintain impeccable relationships.
* Be conscious every moment to put positive thoughts into your mind rather than negative thoughts.
* Appreciate feelings as a means of understanding yourself, thus directing and creating your reality.
* Continue to forgive yourself and others as a means of creating a state of Grace.
* Fill your life with joy and ecstasy by practicing daily the art and skill of verbally expressing your gratitude for all that you have.

Choose wisely to live well.

What Strengthens & Weakens Us

What Weakens Us	What Strengthens Us
Excesses	Moderation
Worry	Blessing
Fear	Trust
Resistance	Release
Judgment	Seeing Good
Pain	Healing
Restriction	Freedom
Hatred	Love
Vengeance	Forgiveness
Anger	Free expression
Lack	Abundance
Littleness	Magnificence
Harshness	Gentleness
Dishonesty	Honesty
Withholding	Openness
Defensiveness	Defenselessness
Impatience	Patience
Stinginess	Generosity
Conflict	Peace
Impotence	Power
Self-denial (martyrdom)	Self-Love
Condemnation	Appreciation

Keys To Fulfillment

1. Recognize and appreciate all you have wanted and experienced in your life, no matter what your judgment.

2. Be willing to release seeming obstacles, limitations, self-sabotage and negative thinking.

3. Move consciousness to a deeper level of quiet mind, creative mind, alpha state, out of fearful, defensive, analytical thought.

4. Allow desires, dreams, hopes and inner vision to come forward.

5. Imagine the fulfillment of all your desires.

6. Trust and believe what is wanted is now being fulfilled.

7. Let go and expect the way and means will be given.

8. Ask for help, support and guidance on the inner and outer.

9. Listen inside and follow explicitly what you hear with gratitude and joyful action.

10. Give thanks at each step of the natural fulfillment of all you desire.

Conceive • Believe • Achieve

How to Achieve True Happiness

Choose to be happy everyday.
Know God's Will is Your Happiness.
Love yourself impeccably.
Love others unconditionally.
Keep yourself full and fulfilled.
Do Good works and live a Godly life.
Give up being right and making others wrong.
Stop fixing or correcting yourself and others.
Give up listening to media negatives.
Let go of telling and believing human drama.
Give what is asked for with gratitude.
Teach with every thought, word and activity.
Model what you want your world to be.
Be true to your highest spiritual principles.
Explore your values and give them priority.
Trust all is well and all you need is given.

Be free.
        Be true.
                Be you.

You Are Enough

Never good enough?
Always needing to be and do and have more?

There is a pervasive cultural belief that we are never enough.
From our childhood we may have received the message, implied or overt, that our Being was not enough to satisfy, to please, to win approval, to be loved by those important in our lives.
When we look to people whose beliefs are limited, lacking and belittling, we learn from their thoughts, words and behavior that they are not enough and we are not enough.

There is always more to do, more to prove, more to achieve, more to earn, more to win, more to get, more to enjoy, more to learn.
What would happen to our ambition and our perfecting, if we knew we were enough?
What would happen to our trying and our achieving, if we knew we have enough?
What would happen to our initiative and our creativity, if we knew we were safe and healed and loved?

You are enough.

You do enough.

You have enough.

Transpersonal Life

When I look at me, what do I see?
When I look at you, what do I see?
When I look at God, what do I see?

When my life is totally to take care of me,
I feel limited and lacking and very little.
I feel vulnerable, alone and inadequate.

When my life is devoted to you,
I am dependent, seek approval & need acknowledgment.
I feel dutiful, responsive and beholden.

When my life is a gift from God and for All Good,
I am part of the whole, the bigger picture.
Everyone is my focus, my friend and my teammate.
I feel fortunate, capable, provided for, and significant.
Every blessing given is a blessing received.

The Transpersonal Life offers an expanded experience of Self in relationship to All.

Every aspect of creation is part of me and I am part of everything.

Everyone is my teacher.

Every thought, word and deed becomes a teaching of Love and a lesson in Love.

I know my part is to be All I Am, everywhere I am and with every One.

I feel grateful, blessed, content and inspired by a greater sense of the Whole of Life.

Who Are You Anyway?

You are as bright as the sun,
    as reflective as the moon,
        as consistent as the stars,
            as gentle as the wind,
                as healing as the rain,
                    as tender as a newborn child.

You are the perfection of a brilliant diamond, smudged and covered in the mud and whitewash of your life journey.

You are the joy of a carousel.

You are the peace of a still pond.

You are the love in a mother's eyes.

You are all this and so much more.

You are what you have been looking for.

No more scavenger hunts or bargain basements.

Look inside to find the treasure you have always sought.

Clear the debris collected in time.

Find what has been missing.

You, the essence of You, hidden and always there waiting, endlessly waiting, for you to claim her and name her.

Never be the same, once you have discovered her.

The gift of You. Always You.

Child of the Infinite,

The Powerful Present of the Most High.

The Wisdom of the Sages.

The Glory of the Ages.

And the Love that never ends.

You, All ways, You.

Cooperation

How do we learn to cooperate with others?
Only when fulfilled, are we fully present.
Only when satisfied, do we deeply care.
Only when truly on purpose, do we really share.
Only when loving ourselves, do we know unconditional love for another.
Only when trusting our inner answers, do we trust another's path.
Only when living in integrity, do we stand in confidence.
Only when walking our talk, do we speak with conviction.
Only when following our dreams, do we inspire others.
Only when we live in harmony and peace, do we create peace with others.
Only when we know we are deeply and profoundly loved, are we truly happy.
Only when we give ourselves permission to explore, do we feel totally free.
Only when we treat ourselves with the best care, are we healthy on all levels.
Only when we are happy and free, do we show others how to be happy and free.
Only when we know we are a winner, do we treat others as winners, too.

Give Your Self always and only the Best.
Everyone will be blessed!

Communication

Honesty

What is honesty? Telling *your truth* as you know it.

What is *your truth*? *Your truth* is seen through your own filters, beliefs, emotions and life experience.

When we believe ours is the only *truth* or position, we are unaware of how perception works. Few people see the world as it is. Some see the world as they want it to be. Most see the world as they fear through their historical and learned perspective. There are infinite perspectives.

There is a story of eight blind men describing an elephant. Each described something totally different, depending on what they felt and heard. All were correct. The work of respectful relationship is to see through another's eyes.

We must seek to understand before being understood. To be "right" about our position is to limit our relationships, to limit our love and to limit our experience of what is. I learned many years ago to recognize and declare my position and then to totally let go and be willing to "not know". This allowed me to really "be with" the other and to see from a broader perspective.

When "being honest" in relationship with yourself or another, I recommend no secrets or withholds, no gossip or stories. Gossip seeks agreement about your perception of another. Secrets set us up for vulnerability. Stories teach others to believe you are your history. Withholds broadcast: "I am afraid you will judge me" and they will. Observe your communication. Notice what you share and withhold. Find your judgments and forgive them. Be willing to look outside of your own box to other viewpoints. Enjoy Being Holy honest and in integrity with the Highest Truth and the Highest Good for all concerned.

There is always more than one individual can know.

Therefore, I cannot judge.

Communication

What is the purpose of all communication?
The essential purpose is to erase all fear and return to Love.
All communication is to restore what is true and loving to our minds so that we can fully appreciate our healed relationships.

<u>Some Tools for Effective Communication:</u>
(If "*Love*" does not work for you, change it to "*Kindness.*")

Practice active, conscious forgiveness of everyone and everything all the time, including ourselves.

Listen within before you speak.
Attune to the Voice of Love in you. Let Love speak to you and through you. Silence your mind as well as your voice, so you can truly hear Love. Listen beneath the words to find the meaning. We are always communicating Love or a call for Love.

Receive the Love that is being given.
There is no need to defend against Love.
"Thank you for loving me."

Respond with Love to the request.
The response may be with words of caring, reassurance or acceptance or it may be silence and a smile.

It is up to the most conscious one to release the fear and really be present.
Be present in an open and accepting state.

Listen within and you will always know how to respond with Love.

Questions To Ask

When someone is needing to make a decision and asks for help or advice, questions are a way of encouraging them to think for themselves and trust their inner knowing. Be sure you are not judging them in anyway, but rather giving them an opportunity to consider more deeply.

Helpful questions we can ask in a neutral way:
What is your intention for doing this?
What is your desired outcome?
What are you losing or gaining?
What may be the effect on others?
Are you hurting or benefiting anyone?
Is there a solution where everyone benefits?
What will be the long range impact?
What do you want for yourself in 20 years?
What are you learning from this?
What are you wanting others to learn?
Are there any mistakes you might be making?
How is this like your previous experiences or patterns?
How are you correcting past mistakes?
Will you have regrets in the future?
Is there a better way to achieve the same outcome?
Is there anything you want to do differently?
Will this decision make you happy?
Will this bring you peace of mind?

From Gossip to Blessing

What if we took all the time and energy we put into gossip (talking about others who are not present) into praying, blessing and affirming. Gossip usually is judgmental of the person or their behavior and activities.

What we perceive and judge in another, we strengthen in ourselves. It rubs off in unconscious ways that often go unnoticed.

Use the creative power of thought to heal and bless.
Give judgments up for prayerful release.
Focus on the highest vision rather than criticize.
Appreciation strengthens.
Criticism and complaints diminish us.
When we have something wonderful to say, say it directly to the person.
When we have a criticism that we are unwilling to share, we must forgive ourselves and pray for kindness and peace.

We are here to offer LOVE.
We are here to forgive our FEAR.
We can quickly forgive our gossiping habit.
We can choose to pray, heal and affirm.
Bless everyone and you will be blessed.

Guidelines For Decisions

When considering any choice or course of action, (especially regarding your primary relationships) ask:

Is it fair?

Is it honest?

Is it beneficial to all concerned?

Does it promote goodwill among all parties?

If not, it will not lead to a healthy and healed relationship.

You may get what you think you want in this moment, but you are likely to create a future relationship issue where you will be treated as you have treated the other.

If your decisions regarding any relationship are fair, honest, beneficial and promote harmony and good will, it is likely you will experience the same treatment in future relationships.

What you give, you receive.
Give only the best you know and you will be assured of receiving the best from others.
Honor your relationships by always choosing what is fair, honest, beneficial and promoting good will.

Teaching Others

We are inviting and teaching others how to treat us by how we treat them.

Am I treating others as I want to be treated?
Am I speaking about others the way I want to be spoken about?
Am I thinking of others the way I want others to think of me?
Am I teaching others the way I want everyone to be?
Is my example one I want to encourage among my friends?

Each one of us is teaching our world by our behavior as well as our words and attitude.
If we are afraid, we may be building a world of fear.
If we are angry, we may be building a world of anger.
If we are discouraged, we may be building a world of despair.

All forgiveness is a gift of peace for ourselves.
All gifts of love are gifts of Love for ourselves.
Acts of kindness are extending kindness to ourselves.

We are worthy of Peace and Love and Kindness, now and always, no matter what we do or say or teach or make.

This is our healing and way to remember Who We Are.

Suggestions For Intimate Sharing

If you want to share with a partner or friend:

Decide the outcome you seek—(peace, happiness, acceptance)

Ask for their time and get permission to share.

Be respectful of their needs to rest, to eat, to handle their own agenda.

Ask specifically for what you want. "*I have some problems or leftover feelings I want to share with you. Is now a good time or is there a better time and place?*"

Be open to their response.

Support their needs as well as your own. A listener is better, when they are prepared and fully available. Don't ask for something the other cannot or does not want to give.

Choose a time and place that is private.

Ask for their listening without comment or ask for what you want from them. Request their agreement. "Are you willing? Is that OK with you?"

Share from your perspective. No blaming or finger pointing. No attack. No accusing them of deceiving you or hurting you. Simply, "*I feel…I want…. I am willing to do …to have what I want….*"

Give the other an opportunity to share without interruption. When you are complete with your sharing, allow them to offer feedback if you can listen without defensiveness.

If you are sharing something you want from them, they may feel hurt and guilty. To increase the chance of them wanting to take responsibility and make behavioral changes, you need to be totally understanding and helpful at this point to encourage them. If you continue to let them know how bad you are feeling, it is more likely they will feel guilty, be defensive and try to hurt and blame you. Or they will feel guilty and hurt and withdraw love and attention from you to heal their wounds.

If you want a win/win solution, it is essential that you clear or heal your own past history first thru journaling, forgiveness or affirmation work. The other person can feel the dump and is ill-prepared to clear it all. They feel attacked and sabotaged.

Dumping everything lets them know you stockpile resentment.

Bringing up past history demonstrates you are unforgiving.

To continue dumping feelings when the other cannot respond, builds resentment and fear in your communication.

Trying to get an apology or behavioral change from the other says they are "wrong" and you are trying to correct them.

This feels belittling and will yield unhealthy results.

Stop yourself, the moment you see the conversation is going awry.

When you are not creating the result of more peace, and understanding, you have erred.

- Stop.
- Look at what just happened.
- Take a break.
- Go be alone.
- Listen inside and write down what you hear.
- *What is making me upset is....*
- *What I can do to become peaceful again is....*
- *What I am trying to heal from my childhood is......*
- *How I can most easily heal and clear this pain is ....*
- Heal from within.
- Then share your learning and healing success with the other.
- You will build confidence, compassion, freedom of expression and Love.

Fighting and Arguing

Arguments or fights usually begin with one person seeking to be right and to making another wrong.
The person bringing up the issue wants the other to take responsibility, to be wrong, to change their behavior or attitude or to feel hurt, too. The initiator usually brings up the issue at a "bad" time, is overwrought with emotion and intends to share their feelings no matter what the other wants. The feelings are often shared in an accusatory or insulting tone which invites the other person to feel guilty and responsible for the problem. The intention is to win and make sure the other guy loses.

The ego is most interested in being right, not in being happy or coming to peace. *Spirit* is always looking for a peaceful resolution in which both are benefited.

When caught up in emotion, the fighter says and does things that are unkind, disrespectful, hurtful and unconscious.
"If I am going to hurt, I will hurt you, too." Most fighters don't realize that the hurt is a product of their hurtful thinking. They make up painful stories or possibilities and then replay them in their own minds until they are wounded and resentful and justified in hurting the other.

Usually the argument has no rules and is a contest to see who can hurt the other the most and is often clever, vicious, manipulative and seductive.
When one person wants to fight to "clear the air", they use the buttons they know to involve the other person. If ignored, they often become mad and offensive about the other being emotionally unavailable. People who are good with words, often use them as a source of power. People who are clever and controlling often use arguments to put the other in their place or teach a lesson or try to get what they want.

Fights and arguments are "no-win" situations.

Neither person is left with their self-respect and dignity. There is often a leftover mess, which is ignored, buried and festers, sometimes for years.

People who like to fight have learned from their childhood, the power of words.

They may actually see arguing as a form of loving and look for the opportunities to "make up".

Fighting is a useless and energy-draining form of relating.

Fights and arguments distract, detour and delay us from finding the source of pain within. Wherever we are blaming, angry or resentful of another, there is always a past source of pain or woundedness that we must access and heal within ourselves.

There is a better way.

Rather than fight or argue, stop and be silent.

Step away and take time to sit with yourself.

Listen within for what is the real reason for the upset.

Write down what you hear inside.

Let your hurt or angry ego or inner child speak.

Let you nurturing or Loving Spirit speak to you.

When you are clear, return to listening with Love.

NO defensiveness.

Only understanding and forgiveness will be present.

Begin Within

What we think about others will be thought about us.
What we say about others will be said about us.
What we do to others will be done to us.
What we think, say and do teaches everyone.
What we perceive in others, we strengthen within ourselves.
What we focus on we create more of.
What we resist or avoid, we give strength to.
What we feed ourselves with media, associations, work and learning,
we become.

We are responsible for giving ourselves the very best so we can teach others to give themselves the very best, so others will give us the very best, so that all humanity will become the very best.

It all begins with you and me, inside our own minds.
I can seek the answers outside, but until they come from me, I will not have the answers.
I can seek love outside myself, but until I love myself all the ways I am, I will not fully believe I am totally loveable.
I can try to change others to get what I want, but until I am what I want to be and give what I want to have, I will not receive what is given by others.
Life is a process of clearing all blocks to the awareness of the presence of Love and Wisdom, Life and Freedom.

It all begins with me.

Love for Others

Special Relationships

All relationships are to heal and remember love, trust and freedom.

When we see ourselves as a body, personality and separate being, we seek someone who will give us the Love we want.

The ego always feels incomplete, seeking for the missing pieces in another person.

The ego sees itself as personality, self-image and body. It seeks another personality in a body to handle the unfulfilled aspects of itself.

*The **True Self** knows Self as whole and complete, happy and free. The **Spirit Self** may be called to partner with another whole and **Holy Being** to serve a Higher Purpose, a True Calling. Their focus and commitment is on Purpose, focused on service to God, and not on each other. No difficulty can shake their commitment, because they are united in Purpose.*

With egoic unions, attraction, fulfillment of the needs, and "falling in love" are what bring couples together. The need for approval and acceptance, security and safety, being needed, being right and looking good are often the goals our little ego self seeks in another.

As long as egos continue to meet the needs of each other, they are committed. When either or both no longer fit the picture, there is disappointment, disillusionment and often disintegration and divorce.

Special relationships often look and feel very safe, secure and comfortable in the beginning. They are based on conditional acceptance. *"As long as you meet my criteria, I will love and accept you. And when you no longer fit my needs, I may judge, hurt, resent, ignore, avoid or get rid of you."*

To transform specialness into healed relationships, forgiveness is required. We are called to forgive and release the past, let go of demands and expectations, forgive ourselves for fears and judgments and forgive others for their unconscious patterns.

Forgiveness is the key.
Relationships are the path to healing, to inner peace, to truly being happy.
When we can treat all relationships with the same respect and consciousness and love all unconditionally, we will see ourselves as whole and Holy, and others as well.
Trust is healing.

Free yourself in the healing process.

Give Your Self to healing your lack of Self Love.

Trust you are here to reveal and heal all the places where you have forgotten to Love You.

Loving You is the door to Lasting Love.

Romantic Relationships

What will you find in romantic relationships?
Most people want to make up for what feels missing.
Most people are seeking to heal the wounds of the past.
Most people want to find the love they never had.
Most people search for what they fantasized.
Most people seek the ideal version of their romantic fantasies.

The problem is that even when you find what you think you want and try to make it yours, it will be ephemeral, coming and going, dependent on the mood, the healing needs, the past history and emotionality of the other. While we seek to get what we want, it will never be lasting and will change according to human condition and emotions.

Specialness

The most common relationship is co-dependent, in which two people come together because their corresponding needs satisfy one another.
They are in a special relationship that will last as long as there is need, as long as they are both needy and dependent on the other for their fulfillment.
Some say over 90% of all relationships are co-dependent. Dependence grows over time, when we deliberately try to meet the needs of the other to gain and maintain a long term relationship.
The world, the job, money and security and our special relationships seduce us into doing and saying and being what we think we have to be, to have and keep what we value.

Whole and Holy Relationships

When two people are whole, conscious, enlightened, responsible and respectful of themselves, their thoughts, words and actions all the time, they need nothing.

Their relationship is guided by their values, choices and intention, rather than emotions and desires.

They are totally honest, trusting, generous, open-minded, defenseless, joyful, faithful, patient and live in integrity with their chosen and expressed values.

They keep their agreements and confer directly when their choices change.

These partners make decisions based on what is fair, caring and sharing.

They are totally responsible for their emotions, thoughts and actions.

They live in a non-blaming and self-affirming state.

They need no one and accept everyone.

They each take full responsibility for the quality of the relationship without guilt or blame.

This rare and unusual relationship is truly "God sent".

What Men and Women Really Want

Generalizations about what gender really wants are just that—generalizations! However there are consistent behaviors among genders that are often misunderstood.

Sometimes men and women simply project their intentions and emotions onto the opposite sex. Or frequently there are gender stereotypes with cause misperceptions when in relationships. i.e. When a woman won't talk, it is because she is resentful or punishing the other person. When men won't talk and withdraw, it is usually because they don't know what to say without exposing their emotional vulnerability and prefer to work it out without hurting the other or themselves.

In general….men simply want to make their woman happy.
Men are simple.
- Men try hard to please the other after doing their "job" the best they can as protector and provider.
- Men are confused by emotions and emotional behavior.
- Men have difficulty reading what changing emotional states and behaviors are really saying.
- Men do their best to make it right, but have limited tools or understanding.
- Men objectify women. Men often are simply seeing their woman as the object of their love.
- Men are dependent on a woman. (Men tend to remarry within one year of losing their partner, On average for women it is five years.)
- Men use their relationship as their north star, the compass by which they guide their course in life.
- Men need their woman to be clear about what really matters and stay true to her word.
- When the woman changes her mind, it is frustrating, confusing and can cause depression and distress.

- Men have learned to stay away when a woman (mother) is upset until they "know" what to do.
- Men try hard to keep the relationship on an even keel.
- Men tend to exert all their energy in doing what they know they can do....earn money and keep safe.
- They often use TV, internet and video games to go into the zone to undo stress and to stay our of trouble.
- In general, criticism shuts down their energy and makes them weak, uncertain and confused.
- Men would rather avoid fights by staying away (under the radar). (Working or playing or unavailable.)
- Men rely on their woman's happiness and approval to know that they are OK, wanted and belong.

In general...women simply want their way.

Women are complex.
- Women please themselves by doing their job of nurturing and nourishing the whole family.
- Women stir emotions and emotional reactions and see them as indicating love and loyalty.
- Women project their motives onto men, not recognizing the differences.
- Women do their best to manipulate, control and convince to get their believed "right" way.
- Women utilize men. Women use men to protect, provide and produce children.
- Women are independent and capable of caring for themselves, but it is less work with willing help.
- Women oversee the big picture and plan for the future of themselves and their families.
- Women multitask and seem to consider all elements.
- Women are best at scheduling and making future plans.
- Women can be effective assistants to men and know how to control the outcome.
- Women use their relationship as the means to get what they want: home, family, travel, companion.

- Women resent criticism and will find ways to get even, defend and attack.
- Women are expecting men to be like women and disrespect men's inabilities to perform.
- Women use emotions and fighting to confuse the man to win and get their way.
- Women use the man's compliance (obedience) as the indication of his love and loyalty.

These **generalizations** are based on 30 years of observation and listening to the genders express their unconscious and conscious motivations.

Make up your own truths, if these are not true for you.

May they be helpful in accepting the differences.

May they bring peace and compassion and understanding to all your relationships.

Love All Equally

To love all equally is to respond with Love to everyone.

To love all equally is to be aware of the inspired guidance and direction within each relationship.

To love all equally is to never quit.

To love all equally is to realize our relationship with God.

To love all equally is not about treating people the same.

Loving everyone equally is not about sexuality, intimacy, helping, living with, or marriage.

Loving all equally is not about praising or agreeing, making special or comparison.

Love is not a behavior or activity. It is realizing Who We Are and the Essence of the other that never changes.

Love is beyond words or deeds, personality or performance.

Loving all equally is learning to love as God loves.

Loving all equally is responding in the moment to what is being called forth. It is about giving to our brother/sister whatever they ask, unless it does harm to them or to us.

Loving all equally is about honoring the Voice within that always helps us choose so that no one loses.

Every relationship is for the purpose of healing the illusions, the guilt, the past, the false, the self-created personality and egoic structures.

To love everyone equally is to know that with total and absolute unconditional Love, all things are healed and return to their natural state of wholeness.

Masculine/Feminine Needs

In most male/female relationships, **the woman is the inspirational leader.** The feminine is most receptive, perceptive and usually has the greatest overview. The masculine component is most focused on accomplishing, providing and doing what obviously needs to be done now. The feminine tends to be more global, social and past/future in focus and the masculine more linear and present. Mostly, the woman tends to be more home-based and the man more work-based. These are generalities and do not fit all gender differences; however, this is the norm and our usual conditioning.

In relationships there is a difference in the roles, functions and responsibilities played by both parties which must be noted and honored to live in harmony.

What are your roles and functions in your relationships? You can choose to change them with full communication and a willingness to learn how to respond to what is needed to build respect, responsibility and cooperation.

To blame the other for some role or responsibility not performed, is to acknowledge that we notice what is missing and refuse to take responsibility. **When we notice a problem or need, it is ours to fill. The conscious one is to respond to what is needed.** When there is an imbalance in the responsibilities assumed in a relationship, it is usually due to the differences in consciousness and learned orientation or perspective.

Usually the male partner focuses on providing, protecting and accomplishing. Usually the female partner focuses on friendships and maintaining the values or spiritual focus of the family system. The cultural norm has shifted dramatically in the last thirty years, so that often men are assigned roles (by women) which are foreign to their nature. As women have taken on more of the traditional male roles, they have blamed men for not taking more of the feminine roles.

Both partners need to be acknowledged and affirmed for what they offer the relationship. To ignore, criticize or expect our partner to do or be more that what comes naturally may undermine the quality of the partnering. We need to recognize we all have learned our roles in male/female relationships from observing our parents, grandparents and other role models in society.

We need to ask ourselves what is natural, what is learned, what is expected, what is judged and choose again for ways that are balanced, fair, honest and good for the whole family system.

Teach gently by being respectful and sensitive to the level of awareness and needs of each person.

Are You in Love?

Are you in Love today?
Have you fallen out of Love with someone?
Have you stopped loving your home or job?
Have you fallen out of love with Life?

Myth: *We need to get love to have Love.*
Myth: *We need to find a special someone to love .*
Myth: *Being in love is chemistry, not a choice.*
Myth: *Falling out of love is not a choice.*

Falling in Love happens when we give ourselves totally to Love and Loving.

Being in Love is experienced when we hold no judgments with the person or the circumstance.
*When we see ourself and others with innocence, we feel **in love**.*
*When we allow ourselves to feel treasured, precious and special, we feel **in love.***
Look into the eyes of the other and allow yourself to see Love reflected there.
Find God, the face of the Divine, in the tender look of the one you are with.
Give yourself time to pause and breathe and say" I Love You", as you end each conversation.

To love as God loves is to fall in Love and be in Love with everyone.

A True Friend

A True friend is a friend in Truth.

A True Friend sees me whole and Holy.

A True friend acknowledges my magnificence.

A True friend encourages my freedom.

A True friend believes the Truth about me, when I have forgotten.

A True friend honors my process and my purpose.

A True friend respects our differences.

A True friend is patient and encouraging.

A True friend accepts me as I Am.

A True friend forgives my mistakes.

A True friend is true to themselves.

A True friend honors my choices.

A True friend responds from their inner guidance.

A True friend sees, speaks and hears no evil.

A True friend is gentle when needed and frank when invited.

A True friend does not sacrifice or martyr.

A True friend accepts rather than expects.

A True friend makes no assumptions.

A True friend keeps their agreements.

A True friend gives their best.

A True friend is willing to let go and love again.

Be a True Friend.

What Works For Me

I live what I am teaching. Robert Waldon and I have shared our lives as spiritual partners for over 27 years. Our focus is on loving unconditionally, serving from the heart and remembering God.

Gifts of Our Holy Relationship:
Willingness to heal all things.
Respect for one another and our life work.
Honoring our individual and joined purpose.
No arguments, anger or resentment.
Healing all guilt with forgiveness.
Treating ourselves with impeccable care.
Spending much silent time everyday.
Conscious quality time together in enjoyment.
Giving All we have for Good.

Practical reminders
Don't criticize. Support one another.
Don't be angry. Be forgiving of yourself.
Don't complain. End each day in gratitude.
Don't feel guilty. Forgive and choose again.
Don't keep silent. Request help in healing.
Don't stay separate. Take time to join in love.
Don't forget to play. Take time to enjoy life.
Don't assume. Be sure to communicate fully.
Don't take upsets personally. Listen with Love.

Family

Mothers' Reminder

If you have nurtured a plant, cared for a pet or created something of beauty, you have "mothered".
We need not gestate and give birth to a child to be a "Mother".
All of us have maternal feelings toward someone or something. This is good and appropriate.
All of us have feminine energies.
All of us have feelings that bring out our protective and nurturing energies.
This is what being a mother is all about.

Love You with a heart that is true and unfailing.
Love You with a love that is unconditional.
Love You with a passion for protection and permission.
Love You with a song that is sweet and reassuring.
Love You with a kindness that is gentle and confirming.
Love You, like a motherless Child.
Love You, like you were the Holy One.
Love You, with kind words and happy thoughts.

If everyone were loved this way, there would be no war, no hate, no violence, no ignorance, no suffering and no pain.
Love Your Self like the very best Mother in the world.

Great Fathers

Give thanks for those who:
Listened to your troubles and gave you a hug.
Believed you could do anything.
Trusted your judgment.
Asked you questions to help you make a decision.
Went to work to provide for your family.
Encouraged your adventures.
Took time to play games and take walks.
Talked with you about God, stars and bigger things.
Knew when to be silent.
Held your hand during difficult times.
Wanted the very best for you.
Cried their tears during special moments.
Received your gifts with enthusiasm.
Found time to attend your special events.
Gave you a call at just the right moment.
Shared their advice and trusted you to decide.
Treated you as an equal.
Helped you learn important stuff.
Encouraged you to figure out how things work.
Gave you a hand when you got stuck.
Were always there blessing you, even now.
We love you Dads, Fathers, Papas, Grandpas and others who play a father role.

Working Together

How do we work together?
To build a successful partnership, a cooperative family, a healthy marriage, a working team:

There must be mutual respect, responsibility and cooperation.
People sabotage their goals with contradictory energies, being at odds within themselves or in their relationships. Whenever there is a force for "yes' and a force for "no", the result is "maybe". A foot on the gas and one on the brakes gets you no where. If you alternate go and stop you have a very slow and jerky ride. Life can work smoothly and easily with integrity and congruence from all parties.

To work together for Good:
There must be agreement about the Good that is being sought.
There must be agreement about the Goal or desired Outcome.
There must be open and honest communication without threat, gossip, secrecy or withhold.
There must be a willingness to give and receive, to teach and learn from one another.
There must be a genuine commitment to an outcome that is Highest and Best for all parties.
There must be responsibility and freedom in the interaction.
Each must care for themselves and their own well-being impeccably.
Each must respond with understanding and acceptance.
Every upset indicates that one has lost their own purpose, and are at the effect of others.
To care for one self is to find and maintain integrity, living and teaching, giving and creating, what is truly the highest vision and goal for ourselves and others.

* Never wish less than the best for others, or you will fear they will do the same for you.
* Never try to win at another's expense, or you will imagine they are doing the same to you.
* Never gossip about or hold judgments against others, or you will fear they are judging you.
* Never say you want respect, but treat the other disrespectfully, or you will beget disrespect for yourself.
* Never give what you don't want to receive, for you will receive it.

Such is the metaphysical law of reciprocity.

Always give your highest and best to everyone in all circumstances.

You will teach others to live with respect, responsibility and cooperation.

Build teamwork everywhere.

Parenting Teens

How long does it take to rebuild trust after your teen has made errors in judgment?
You no longer have the same control or power as when your child was younger. It is an appropriate time for values clarification as he matures into a young adult.
You can parent him as a restrictive and protective parent.
You can parent as a lenient and permissive parent.
You can recognize him as equal and relate with mutual respect.

Assess your level of communication now.
Be conscious of your degree of respect for one another?
If not, you have some relationship building to do.
If so, it is time to listen to his self-made rules, guidelines, boundaries and consequences.

Ask your teen:
What are reasonable guidelines for you?
What are reasonable consequences of breaking those rules?
What are the rights and responsibilities for a teenager?
What are the rights and responsibilities of the parent?
How can I best support you in making wise choices?
How can you support me in trusting and respecting your choices?

Remember Parents:

You are a conscious, conscientious and respectful Being.
You are a wise, discerning, honest teacher of Love.
Your teen is your student and your teacher as well.
Every family member is a guest in your home.
Treat him as such and you will be amazed at the results.
Respect and responsibility with freedom is a great teacher of Unconditional Love in all families.

Build Strong Families

When building a strong family or community, some building blocks are needed. Most people join together without ever considering the essentials.

The family may fall apart because it was not built with a substantial foundation for success.

People or membership: *Who is included and what are their qualifications and functions?*

Space: *How much space is needed and how is it designed and designated and for whom?*

Responsibilities: *What are the guidelines to create community and family fairness and responsibility?*

Finances: *How much money is needed? How is it received and how is it distributed and shared?*

Decision-making: *What is the line of authority? Who makes and implements decisions? Authoritative or democratic?*

Conflict-Resolution: *With disagreement, how do the individuals come to resolution, respect and understanding?*

These areas must be clarified, communicated and agreed upon to maintain the integrity and success of the family and community.

Where you have awareness, you can heal.

Where you forgive, you can begin again.

Where you see lack, you can bring wholeness.

Make a decision to create with solid building blocks that support the Good of All.

Seek The Highest

Whom do you admire?
To whom do you go for counsel?
Who do you know who lives well?
Who do you respect for their goodness?
In whom do you believe and trust?

When you seek for a model or example, always look to the Highest. Never settle for the ordinary.

Look at the people, places and lives you value. Admire, appreciate, contribute, validate, enjoy and value what you want more of in your own life.

This will grow the good. This will enhance your values. This will open the door to learning. This will demonstrate the ways and means, the 'how to's' for you.

When you want knowledge and wisdom, go to the teacher who lives what they teach.

Seek out the minister who practices what he preaches.

Ask for healing from the healer who is whole and heals from within.

Spend time with the Holy man who values your Holiness.

This is the way to enlightenment.

This is the way to satisfy your soul.

Association enhances remembering what you want to live and give.

Sacred Assignments

When was the last time you thanked your mother?
When have your told your father you loved him?
When did you last hug your children?
When did you last genuinely appreciate your partner.

Life gives us assignments: people who need our love, our forgiveness, our healing. These relationships may feel like **projects** for which we have to set goals and priorities, work with patience and persistence to succeed.

We may expect something coming from the other.

We complain about how little we have received.

We may judge the other as inadequate, flawed or wrong.

As children of our parents, we think they owe us something. What can they give but what they have?

Often the patterns of loving and giving have been faulty and lacking for generations.

It is up to the most conscious one. *Are you not that One?*

The conscious One is here to <u>give</u>.

You are here to give to those who are lacking.

You are here to love those who are fearful.

You are here to heal those who are wounded.

You are here to forgive those who are guilty.

You are here to comfort those who are suffering.

You are here to bring solace to the grieving.

You are here to offer gentleness to the cruel.

You are here to give Love to the loveless.

It is in giving that you receive.

It is in giving that you receive the gifts you give.

It is in giving that you recognize the gifts you have.

It is in giving that you teach others to give.

It is in giving that we realize....

LIFE IS FOR GIVING.
WE ARE THE GIFTS, ONE TO ANOTHER.

What Our Children Want

What do our children need from us?
What is our responsibility to our children?
What do our children really want?

Our children want Peace not war.
Our children want Love, not fear.
Our children want Freedom, not limitation.
Our children want Power, not impotence.
Our children want Joy, not sorrow.
Our children want Presence, not our busyness.
Our children want Trust, not our doubt.
Our children want Compassion, not our judgment.
Our children want Listening, not our lectures.
Our children want Time, not our money.
Our children want to Live, Laugh, and be Happy.

Is this not the same as every one of us wants?

Are we not all Children of the Universe?

Challenges

The 5 Languages of Fear
The 5 Calls for Love

*An intuitive look at some possible explanations
for unacceptable behavior.*

According to <u>A Course in Miracles</u>, everything is either a gift of love or a call for love. The 5 Languages of Love (Dr. Gary Chapman) teach us more about how to effectively give and receive the **gifts** of love, but what about responding to the **calls** for love? The answer is always to "give love", but that is only possible **after** we have stopped reacting to the call as a personal attack. **The first step is awareness.**

Awareness with love is healing.

When people are in fear or pain (and needing love), they are not always sensitive, aware, articulate, considerate or even caring. They will either see you as the cause of their current dilemma or just a handy (loving) person they can strike out at so they won't be alone in their misery. They will either deprive you of what they know you value most or what they, themselves, value most.

Here are 5 possible disguises of the call for love.

1. The Put-Down—This includes complaining, anger, blame, guilt, insults, destructive words. If Words of Affirmation are a primary love language for you, **hearing** someone else's pain directed at you can be especially hurtful.
2. The Cold Shoulder—This includes being pre-occupied, too busy, multi-tasking, distracted, walking away, ignoring, threatening to leave or end the relationship, shutting you out. If Quality Time is a primary love language for you, being left alone or **abandoned** can be devastating.
3. The Take-Away—This includes taking or breaking things, stealing, constantly saying "We can't afford it", not giving or sharing, being selfish. If Receiving Gifts is a primary

love language for you, being **deprived** will be hurtful way out of proportion to the value of the actual gift itself.

4. The Complication—This includes forgetting to do things, being too busy to help out, refusing to help, being destructive, making messes, causing problems, adding complications and making more work. If Acts of Service are a primary love language for you, the **burden** of having to do more or do it all yourself leaves you feeling hurt and resentful.

5. The Hurt—This includes hitting, hurting, outside affairs and cheating, withholding/denying touch and affection, and all acts of physical violence. If Physical Touch is a primary love language for you, either **destructive touching** or **touch deprivation** can cause you to emotionally wither and want to withdraw from the world.

Keys to responding with love:

1. **Don't take it personally.** It's not about you. It's about them. If you take it personally, they may think it actually **is** about you and fail to (eventually) take responsibility for their condition.

2. **Take care of yourself.** You may need to actually remove yourself from the situation in order to stop getting hurt and to get clear. If you let them hurt you, you create either conscious or unconscious guilt on their part, which will cause them to either attack more vigorously or withdraw completely.

3. **Listen within for guidance.** Once you can bring yourself to peace and neutrality, listen to your heart about how to respond. This is clearly a call for love. What does the other person actually need or want that will be most easily received by them. Do you need to speak, write, think, pray, act?

4. **Do what you hear and trust it is good.** Get on with your life and keep loving yourself so you can continue to love others.

When Upset

I am never upset for the reason I think.

Being upset means:
I have lost my center.
I have forgotten my Holiness.
I have forsaken my Peace of mind.
I have given value to something other than Source.
I have taken something personally.
I have attacked myself with my interpretation.
I have judged falsely.
I have not remembered to give love.
I have chosen to react rather than respond.
I have set myself up for failure.
I have sabotaged my own wholeness.
I have made up that someone is attacking me.
I have chosen to hurt myself.
I have forgotten to trust God.
I neglected to listen within and follow my Inner Voice.

Whether upset shows up with anger and blame, regret and sorrow, pain and confusion, I have lost my Center of Peace.

I forgive myself for forgetting and choose again.
I am now centered in Peace and balanced in Love.

Mistakes

Our way to feel confident and equal in all our relationships is to live our Best and give our Best.

Where we forget to give our best, we feel less.

Where we live less than we know to be good for us, we feel cheated and guilty.

We may blame someone, because we don't want to take responsibility for our choices.

Blame and criticism are <u>always</u> a sign that we lost our Center and our Purpose.

Blame and criticism are always guilt projected onto others.

The innocent or natural response to an error is to acknowledge our mistake, let it go with gratitude for the learning and choose again for the best we know.

As adults we learn to cover our mistakes with justification, blame others for our choices, and maintain our unconsciousness.

Adulteration teaches us to look good and be right.

All Mistakes are learning opportunities.
I easily let go and choose again.
I forgive myself for blaming anyone.
I am willing to make good choices.
I learn from everything and everyone.
Forgiveness is easy and natural for me.
I remember to love myself no matter what.

Sacrifice or Sacred?

Have you sacrificed for others?

Do they feel appreciative or guilty for your sacrifice?

When we give our selves, our heart and soul for another or a project, our appreciation indicates the gift has been received.

Our guilt indicates our martyrdom. The gift loses its value to giver and receiver.

In some cultures guilt is the price of love.

Where there is guilt, there is resentment. Where there is guilt and resentment, there is a need for healing, forgiveness and Love.

Sacrifice means "to make sacred."

Make all your gifts and giving sacred for you and the recipient.

All that we give is a gift to ourselves.

Make sure that what you are giving is a gift in the giving and that you need nothing in return.

To lay down one's life for another is a true gift only when we are lifted up and inspired in the giving.

To suffer and martyr ourselves is perceived by the other as producing guilt and reluctance to receive the gift.

Give your gifts with no conditions, purely for the joy of giving.

Let others know there is no sacrifice, but rather it is a privilege to give, to love and to serve.

Relationship Stress

Relationships are about creating connections.
To connect means we see, know and value the other as much as ourselves.

Relationships are about loving with trust and freedom.
To love is to trust in the other's process and to freely accept the other as they are.

Relationships are for healing our past unfinished business.
Healing comes from awareness with non-judgment.
The ego self responds to relationship stress with **intimidation** (blame and threats), **interrogation** (questions and doubts), **withdrawal** (aloof and silent treatment), **victimization** (sickness and poor me). Egoic behavior yields less intimacy, separation and lack of love.
The Spiritual Self responds to relationship stress with **forgiveness, willingness to listen and learn, taking total responsibility, respect and gratitude.** Spiritual behavior yields connection and intimacy, closeness, and fulfillment of Love.

Building trust means developing patterns of behavior that are respectful and appreciative of the other.
Learning to really listen requires work, taking time, eye contact, confidentiality, no interruptions, no blame.

Unfair Treatment

When it feels as though you were treated unfairly, blamed unjustly, served unconsciously, used without gratitude or taken advantage of, what do you do?

When an agreement is made and promises are not met, how do you respond?

Do you put up with it?

Do you take care of it yourself?

Do you forgive and forget?

Do you speak up?

Do you take responsibility?

Do you complain?

Do you feel hurt?

Do you let go and move on?

Do you gossip about the person or problem?

Do you learn how to communicate clearly?

Do you improve your discernment?

In each instance of unconscious omission or commission or conscious omission or commission, **it is up to the most conscious one to respond.**

When you see a problem, stop any reactivity, look at the whole experience objectively, listen within to your inner voice and respond with what is for the Highest Good of all concerned. To go unconscious in an unconscious world leads to more sleeping minds, ignorant behavior, and unloving feelings. *It is up to you to bring the light and awareness that opens the way for more conscious responses.*

I choose to never teach others guilt or fear.

I choose to bring clarity and consciousness.

I choose to respond in a helpful way.

I choose the Highest Good for All concerned.

I choose to trust everyone is learning.

I choose to serve my Peace of mind.

Asking For Help

Is it OK to ask for help and support?
Is it OK to ask for healing and love?
Is it OK to ask for appreciation and thanks?
Is it OK to ask for livelihood and money?
Is it OK to ask for affection and friendship?
In healthy relationships, it is essential to ask.
In honest relationships, we must tell our truth.
It is loving to ask for what we want.
People can say "No" without losing our love.
People can say "No" without guilt or fear.
Those who ignore a request often deny their own requests. They may ignore their own needs and fear asking others.
Those who get angry, when they receive a request, may feel guilty or afraid of their own desire to say "No".
Those who get angry may feel guilty about not giving what is being asked. Those who get angry may blame the asker for not being independent and self-sufficient. Those who get angry may feel there is no need to ask, since they judge the other has enough.
To make your request:
It is important to ask without demand or obligation.
It is important to ask without threat or fear.
In response to a request:
It is important to say "No" without guilt or anger.
It is important to say "No" with respect and love.
It is important to say "Yes" with joy and gratitude.
Whatever a brother or sister asks, give it, unless it does harm to him or to you. The Golden Rule: "***Do unto others as you would have them do unto you.***"
Bless your willingness to ask.
Bless your willingness to receive.
Bless your willingness to say "No".
Bless your willingness to say "Yes" with Joy.

Falsely Accused

Have you been falsely accused?
Have you been unjustly punished?
Have you been wrongly criticized?
Have your been unfairly rejected?
Some say it is Karma. Past payback.
Some say it is darkness attracted to Light.
Some see it as guilt projected onto Innocence.
Where there is comparison, there may be jealousy and attack.
Whatever the cause, **Forgiveness and Love are always the answer.
Never let anyone or anything harm you.**
If someone pushes your buttons, be grateful for knowledge of the button. Heal the button. Take nothing personally. The criticism, rejection or blame always comes from one who is self critical, guilty or self-rejecting. If what they have to say can be helpful to you, use it with gratitude and respect. If not, offer blessing, forgiveness and contribution. Blaming, criticizing or rejecting the other only leads to more of the same.
Taking it personally and being hurt leads to more abusive behavior and guilt for the other. This is not healing or helpful.
How to respond?
Listen within. When you have handled your own feelings, you may be called to apologize for any hurt or offense you may have caused unconsciously. You may be called to ask what you can do to bring the situation to a peaceful conclusion. You may be called to state your High Truth, i.e. *"My intention is to respect and support you in whatever is best for you."* You may be called to silently say a prayer and do nothing overtly. You may be called to withdraw your energy and offer it where you are valued and respected.
Listen within. Be as a child.
Trust what you hear and know inside.
Take impeccable care of yourself.

Arguments

Arguing is unnecessary and valueless.

Arguing is to make the other wrong and be right.
In either case, we are attempting to win at another's expense. It is "I win" and "You lose". Whenever anyone loses, feels attacked, embarrassed, the relationship loses. Whenever we make ourselves right at another's expense, we lose their respect and cooperation.

Arguing will lessen the bank account of trust between two people.

It takes two to argue. One can stop the cycle of fighting and arguing.

Sharing one's opinion one time is enough.
There is no need to nag.
There is no need to push for agreement.
There is no need to make the other feel guilty.
There is no need to explain, justify or prove.
There is no need to get your way.
There is no need to finish on top.

To complete each day with peace is most important.
To finish the day with "I love you and I know you love me." is essential.
To complete your interaction with mutual trust and respect is valuable.

Arguing is unnecessary and valueless for those who seek peace, happiness and lasting love.

Clearing Attack

Have you felt attacked, criticized, or scape-goated?
Have you felt hurt, betrayed, rejected or abandoned?

Awareness with non-judgment heals.

Look for patterns.
Has this happened before?
When was the first time?
What is you earliest memory?
What was your reaction or response?
What did you believe then?
What was the decision you made?
How can you see it all differently?
What is the decision you want to make now?

Remember:
Fear attracts fear.
Judgment attracts judgment.
Love blesses.
Forgiveness heals.

Truths:
Those who attack are hurting.
Those who feel attacked are hurting.
Those who are hurting need healing.
Forgiveness and kindness heal.

May all be kind to each other.

Love Is Letting Go

When is it time to go?
-When there is completion.
-When there is mutual respect.
-When teaching and learning are done.
-When there is no harm.
-When all is fair and honest.
-When no one loses.
-When there is peace.
-When Spirit shows you the way.
When you Love, you set others free.
When you Love, letting go is natural.
When you Love, you seek to give not get.
When you Love, you free not bind.
When you Love, you support All equally.
When you Love, you know All is well.
When you Love, you respect others' wishes.

Is it time for you to let go?
Love is letting go of fear.
Love never ends, while it may change form.
Love is infinite and Eternal.

"I loose you and let you go. It is done and over."
"I let go and let God."
"I forgive you and bless you."
"I release you to your Highest Good."
"I choose to forgive myself and all others for hurting me."
"I choose to take good care of my whole self now."
"I forgive the past. I forgive the present. I forgive the future. "I am free
to choose what is best for me right now. I do so with Love."

Let go with forgiveness and peace.

Ouch! Attachments!

Wherever there is attachment, there is potential for pain and suffering. Wherever there is need and longing, even passion for something or someone, there is attachment.

The Buddhists say, *"Attachment is the source of all suffering."* Non-attachment is the key. Where we really want or need something to be so, there is potential for it not to be so. Thus we are vulnerable to pain in this world of attachment to illusion, a temporary and ever-changing state of being and relating. Most humans are really attached and dependent on things, events and people. The state of worry, anxiety, pain, and frustration can be almost constant. The experience of true contentment and happiness is illusive at best. When we allow ourselves to release and let go, we discover more inner peace. As we trust in the Higher Truth beyond what seems to be, we find freedom from fear and worry. As we have fewer attach-ments, they may seem even more painful and problematic because of the extreme contrast with our normal peaceful state.

There is value in recognizing what is ailing us:

We have forgotten to trust.

We have made up the way we want our world to be.

I forgive pain and suffering.

I forgive my attachments.

I forgive my need to change.

I forgive my un-peace.

I forgive my guilt and sorrow.

I forgive my thinking and worrying.

I forgive my wishing and trying to change things.

I forgive everyone and everything, including me.

I choose to trust in Good and in God.

I choose to be free and happy.

I choose to Peace.

I choose to Love.

I choose to remember "All is Well."

Reaching Out With Love

How do you love someone who is angry, depressed, scared or hurting?
How do you reach out to someone who is hiding, withholding, defensive, or belligerent?
How do you help someone who is self-effacing, destructive, negating or in denial?
How do you help, when you care and want to make someone happy and healthy and whole?
What do we do when we want to fix the ills in our world and the lack of peace and happiness in our family.

We can ask what they want from us when they come seeking. We can offer suggestions and our own personal advice.

We can listen and be present through the tears and rage.

We can hold and reassure, give comfort and compassion.

We can refer to others by recommending help we believe in. We can honor their process and trust in their sacred journey. We can acknowledge that we do not know what to do.

We can push and prod, demand and plead.

We can give it all to God in prayer and walk away in faith.

We can love them no matter what.

We can give them what we would want to have.

We can forgive ourselves for judging their problems.

We can erase our own fears and needs to fix or cure.

We can know all is well, no matter how it appears.

We can be whole and happy and at peace.

I cannot know what is Good for the other. I forgive my own fear-based opinions and judgments. I listen within to Holy Spirit and do and say as I feel guided. I honor that there is a Higher Power and Purpose that is beyond my understanding. My work is to come to Peace and give from the core of my Being the Highest and Best I know.

Your Feelings Are Invitations to Heal

All upsets are past similars. You are upset by an earlier experience that was never resolved, healed or understood. Being upset is a wakeup call to see where you have forgotten your Essence, lost your purpose and have become a "victim". Being hurt is an indication that you have taken another's behavior or words personally. Being offended is an indication that you have a wound, a place of vulnerability that is calling for your own compassion and self healing.

When you are upset, it is helpful to stop, notice and give positive attention to clear your upset. Take time alone. Ask yourself, "*What is upsetting you? What do you want?*"

You may need time to sit and listen and write your feelings. You may want to be heard to be able to get to the bottom. To express your feelings to the one who pushed your buttons will not yield neutral listening, so step away and write to yourself. You will find at the bottom of all upsets are historical patterns of feeling hurt or blamed by others' behavior or words.

What do you need to heal those thoughts and feelings?

Offer forgiveness.

Ask to see it all differently.

Ask to see from the other's perspective.

Ask to let go and love again.

Ask to release your sensitivity and emotional button.

Ask to be the conscious one and learn from the experience. Forgive yourself for letting anyone or anything harm you.

You may wish to return to the other and share with them your personal healing process. It is always valuable to thank them for pushing your button or upsetting you so you know what you need to heal. You will feel grateful to them, when you have done the inner healing work. You will continue to feel anger, hurt, fear and resentment, until you do the inner work to help and heal yourself.

Heal Your Own Upsets.

Dealing With Difficult People

Remember: We cannot change anyone.
We can change ourselves!

1. Take care of yourself first.
    Be positive and responsive in the moment.
2. Allow no one to harm you.
    Where there is no harm, there is no blame.
3. Express yourself clearly. *"I feel ____*
    when you do ___ and I would prefer _____."
    i.e.: "I feel disappointed when you are late and I want respect."
    "I feel hurt when you yell, and I prefer you talk with me."
4. State your opinion and/or desire one time with feeling.
    No nagging.
5. Listen to the other's ego responses and honor their deeper feelings
    with respect.
6. Provide the holding, safety, and warmth in which the other can
    heal and grow.
7. Visualize the other in a positive light.
    See them free of fear and guilt and at peace.
8. Affirm their wholeness and holiness beneath the personality and
    ego.
9. Give the relationship to Spirit.
    Trust in the perfect outcome.
10. When in doubt, use the Serenity Prayer.
    "God, Grant me the serenity to accept the things I cannot change,
    the courage to change the things I can, and the wisdom to know
    the difference."

Emotional Pain

Emotional pain is not caused by another's behavior or words.
It is caused by our interpretation and reaction to the other.

When we have the mistaken belief that others cause our pain, we believe and experience pain from others' words of unkindness, carelessness, blame, fear and woundedness.

When we hear another's words of lack of Love, we interpret their unlovingness as being our fault. We feels blamed, hurt, guilty and frightened of being rejected . When we learned in childhood that we were responsible for our parents' unhappiness, we imagine the same to be true with loved ones who are expressing their unhappiness. Our mind may interpret all expressions of lack of love as being our fault.

Our healing is to forgive ourselves for not remembering to respond with love.
Our healing is to forgive ourselves for being hurt or frightened.
Our healing is to give our very Best.
Our healing is to listen with peace and Love in our hearts.
Our healing is to flush the poison and extend Love.
Our healing is to be at peace.
Our healing is to not make assumptions about what is needed. Our healing is to not take on another's pain.
Our healing is to let go and Love again.

Love never fails.

More Is Needed

When your relationship feels strained, flat, conflicted, uncertain or just 'not right', MORE of YOU is needed.

* More loving and giving,
* More listening and learning,
* More intimacy and sharing,
* More touching and affection,
* More appreciation and affirming,
* More forgiveness and sensitivity,
* More helpfulness and responsibility,
* More seeking what is best for the other.

It is up to the most conscious one to attend to what is missing.
When we have given to ourselves with love and respect, our response-ability is to give to others with love and respect.
If we are depleted, fatigued, hurt, guilty or angry, we interact with the other in ways that imply our neediness, and wanting others to "fix" our problem.
When we are conscious, we are to heal from within, and then reach out with Love, Trust and Freedom.

If you know what is wanted and needed, do it.

If you don't know what is needed, ask!

Every relationship deserves your very best.

Trust your intuition and give from your heart.

Creating What You Want

To have the relationships we want, apply seven key steps. The steps apply to all relationships, even those that are difficult.

Vision- See clearly in your imagination what it is you want. To see what is wrong only promotes more of the same. See your ideal in great detail and with enthusiasm.

Faith- Believe that it is possible and is awaiting you right now. What you believe is possible for you, you will see. Beneath the surface of what appears to be real is your heart's desire.

Passion- To have what you desire , you must have the courage to want what you really want without compromise or quitting. Invite your ideal with all your heart and all your mind.

Commitment- To achieve success in actualizing any dream, goal or vision, one must be totally committed to persist until success and fulfillment are achieved. 100% commitment without quitting always yields ultimate success.

Strategy- The planning to fulfill your dream is best done by the Highest within you. Listen within on a moment-by-moment basis to what is being called forth. Trust only in love-based guidance and solutions.

Action- Be willing to boldly act on what you hear and know from deep within. Your soul calls you to live an abundant life of actualization of your whole Self . This includes all your relationships which serve your healing and fulfillment.

Gratitude- Celebrate the Purity of your intention, the Innocence of your faith, the Beauty of your vision, the Joy of your inner listening and the Enthusiasm of your action.

You can have what you really want.
Take your foot off the brakes.
Eliminate the "if's" in your commitment.
Clarify the qualities of your vision rather than the details of form.
Honor your heart.
What you seek to achieve is yours for the asking.

Tools

Recommendations for Successful Relationships

This applies to mates, partners, friends, children, co-workers.

Keep your agreements faithfully.
(Communicate changes honestly and immediately.)
Give more than you expect to receive.
Do more than your "fair" share.
Receive everything with open appreciation.
Express your thanks sincerely and take nothing for granted.
Live your own life in integrity and on purpose.
Clarify, communicate and live your mission, your path, your principles and values.
Be responsible for yourself, your work and live your life impeccably.
Don't expect others to pick up after you or take care of you.
Stop using, blame, criticism or guilt to control or manipulate.
Stop making demands, threats or using neediness to get your way.
Communicate effectively and respectfully.
Request a time and place and tone of voice that works for both parties.
Be your best self in all circumstances.
Focus always on teaching by example. (and apologize immediately when you forget or neglect.)
Use your time together wisely.
Focus on meaningful, positive and inspiring conversation and activities.
Spend time, money, energy and resources only on what you value and want to increase.
Waste nothing in your relationship. No arguing, pettiness, emotional dumping or negativity.

Relationship Truths

All relationships are for the purpose of teaching and learning.

All relationships are reminders of what we believe.

Relationships offer what we need to remember who We Are.

There are no accidental encounters.

What we give, we receive.

What we believe, we shall see.

What we think and say and do is teaching everyone.

Relationships are mirrors of what we need to see, forgive and choose differently.

We are here to heal our relationships.

We are here to be truly helpful in our relationships.

We are here to learn to always give our very best.

We are here learn not to take other's pain personally.

We are here to let Love lead the way.

We are here to extend blessing and love to everyone.

What we hold inside our minds radiates out to other minds.

My responsibility is clearing my mind and opening my heart.

Whatever is not Love is always a call for Love.

My vocation is to recognize and release all blocks to the awareness of Love.

Love is freedom and trust. (Freedom to learn in our own timing and way. Trust that Love is our natural state)

My function is to forgive everything that "inter-fears" with extending Love. We are here to forgive mistakes and bless the essential Goodness in All. When we love and respect ourselves, we can easily love and respect others.

We are here to learn to Love, no matter what.

Love is Who We Are.

Love is our natural state.

When we forget to Love, we have lost our True Identity.

The only mistake we ever make is when we forget to Love.

Unconscious Patterns of Relationships

Anything unresolved with parents
will come up in our relationships

1. We tend to recreate our parent personality type in other relationships.
2. We tend to recreate the kind of relationship we had with our parents in our other relationships.
3. We tend to copy the relationship our parents had with each other by acting out their roles in order to understand and justify their behavior.
4. We tend to create upsets to get disapproval from our partners as our parents disapproved of us.
5. We tend to get even with our parents by having relationships that they won't accept.
6. We tend to seek relationships to play helpless, to be in control by being a child, wanting the other to be our parent.
7. We tend to recreate the same degree of struggle in our relationships as we had in our family pattern.
8. We tend to bring our suppressed sexual feelings from childhood into our relationships and feel inhibited sexually.
9. We tend to attract a partner who fits all our patterns.

We attract what we're accustomed to.
We interpret others' behaviors as being the same as in our family patterns.
We cause or create behavior we're used to.
We leave relationships which are too easy or good or which don't fit our patterns.
(From Loving Relationships Training, Sondra Ray)

Possible Purposes For Relationship

1. To give and receive love

2. To learn how to be truly loving

3. For safety and security

4. Companionship

5. To support one another's highest potential

6. To create a happy, loving family

7. To contribute to the well being of others

8. Divine Will—Serving God

9. To heal the past, free us from childhood pain

10. Partnership to accomplish something—Joining for a higher purpose

11. Self knowledge

12. Growth and learning

13. To discover God

14. To fulfill Divine mission or plan

15. To teach what we need to learn

16. Understanding and loving God

17. Learning forgiveness

18. To have someone to play with

19. To have someone to keep us on track

20. To experience joining on many levels

What is true for you?

Partnership Agreements

I encourage you and your partner, together, to write out all of your agreements.
I encourage all parties to take time to re-evaluate your agreements monthly or on a regular basis.

As circumstances change, there is a need to re-commit to what works for all participants.
Families need to meet to look at the specific needs of each individual to be at their best.
Couples need to ensure that the relationship is "serving all parties.
Business partners need to return to their original agreement and consider changing roles as needed.

Life requires that we be in relationship.
With respect for ourselves and each other there is open communication.
With responsibility for the quality of our relationships, there is a willingness to seek what works for all.
With cooperation there is encouragement to listen for ways to serve the needs of everyone.
When everyone WINS, the relationships are harmonious, peaceful and enjoyable.

Blessings to us all in our willingness to continue to explore and find better ways of relating.

Basics For Fulfillment

Respect:
Learn to respect your Self and respect your partner. Listen with patience. Look beneath the surface and see the Essence, the undiscovered treasures.

Gratitude:
Develop an attitude of gratitude and admiration for your partner. Look for what is Highest and Best. Value the gift of the other's wisdom, compassion and sharing with you. Appreciate being in relationship.

Forgiveness:
Acknowledge any judgments you have of your relationship. Forgive yourself for being judgmental. Let go of criticism and seek anyway to encourage.

Willingness:
Be willing to be flexible, forgiving, patient and kind. Be willing to be the one to remember to love when it seems love, gratitude and respect have been forgotten. Be willing to never quit on love.

Responsibility:
Take responsibility for your experience of the relationship. Actively seek opportunities to offer the inner wisdom, spiritual guidance, and Presence needed in difficult situations. Take responsibility for what seems needed to benefit All.

Love or Infatuation?

Infatuation is instant desire.

It is one set of glands calling to another.

Love is friendship that has caught fire.

It takes root and grows—one day at a time.

Infatuation is marked by feelings of insecurity. *You are excited and eager, but not genuinely happy. There are nagging doubts, unanswered questions, little bits and pieces about your beloved that you would just as soon not examine too closely. It might spoil the dream.*

Love is the quiet understanding and mature acceptance of imperfection. It is real. It gives you strength and grows beyond you—to bolster your beloved. You are warmed by his presence, even when he is away. Miles do not separate you. You want him near. But, near or far, you know he is yours and you can wait.

Infatuation says, "We must get married right away. I can't risk losing him/her."

Love says, "Be patient. Don't panic. He/she is yours. Plan your future with confidence."

Infatuation has an element of sexual excitement. *If you are honest, you will admit it is difficult to be in one another's company unless you are sure it will end in intimacy.*

Love is the maturation of friendship. *You must be friends before you can be lovers.*

Infatuation lacks confidence. *When he/she is away, you wonder if he/she is cheating. Sometimes you even check.*

Love means trust. You are calm, secure and unthreatened. He/she feels that trust and makes him/her even more trustworthy.

Infatuation might lead you to do things you'll regret later, but love never will.

Love lifts you up. *It makes you look up. It makes you think up. It makes you a better person than you were before.*

Paradoxes of Relationship

1. In order to be close, there must be space.

2. The only way to have a relationship is to let go.

3. You can only give to another when you have given to yourself first.

4. You cannot truly be in a marriage until you recognize the part of you that wants out.

5. Commitment goes hand-in-hand with freedom.

6. You have more power when you discontinue manipulating and controlling your partner and allow freedom of choice.

7. People are stronger when they allow their weaknesses to show.

8. Acceptance of the mate and the relationship "as it is" is the most effective way to growth and change.

9. Awareness and expression of negative aspects is more conducive to growth than denial and repression of them.

10. The more we become aware of our differences, uniqueness and separation, the more connection and intimacy we can achieve in our relationships.

(Note: This material comes from A New Blueprint for Marriage. This book is currently out of print, but may be found in the library.)

Principles For Living

Our global family needs us.
Our principles must lead us.
Our history precedes us.
Our Love and Trust must free us.

What can you do?
Make a list of your values.
Prioritize your values.
The top 5-10 values must fill every aspect of your life.
Values determine what we experience and what we have. When we are living in alignment with our values, our lives work.
When we forsake our values, we betray ourselves. causing self doubt and lack of confidence.
We weaken ourselves and become less effective at everything we do.

Make a list of the principles you live by.
What are the ideal guidelines you set forth to follow in everyday interaction?
Use your principles for decision-making and conflict resolution.
How do you remain true to your own core beliefs?
When you have discovered the principles that are True for you, live them everyday in everyway and you will strengthen your own integrity and character.

Life works when we do the work.

Perception

Perception is a mirror, not a fact.

What we see in another is a projection of our history and our internal judgments. We see what we want to see, what fits with our current ideas, beliefs, and attitudes.

Relationships are an opportunity to become a spotless mirror.

Relationships show us where we are stuck in opinions and self-judgment.

Healing our perceptions, clearing our relationships, loving everyone equally, and cleaning our mirror is the purpose of the world and physical experience.

Present moment experiences reflect past similars.

We recreate past patterns until we clear misperceptions.

Most relationships with lovers, spouses, children, employers and friends are to heal and clear the past.

Awareness with no judgment is healing.

We are responsible for our experience and receive what we have asked for exactly as we have asked.

Everything works together for good.

To the degree we respect ourselves,
> **we are respected by others.**

To the degree we abandon ourselves,
> **we are abandoned by others.**

To the degree we listen to and honor ourselves,
> **we are listened to and honored by others.**

To the degree we love and trust ourselves,
> **we can love and trust others.**

This is the healing for relationships. The simple truth is that the outer reality is a reflection of our inner experience.

Undoing Blocks To Love

Heal your love for your parents.
Clear your guilt and fear.
Trust God's Will for your happiness.
Live in the present moment.
Release the past.
Listen to your inner voice in what to say.
Open yourself to enjoy what you have.
Be defenseless.
Give up the need to be right.
Be willing to see where you are unwilling.
Acknowledge what you want and ask for it.
Learn to love, appreciate and honor yourself.
Be grateful that you have someone to love.
Give yourself what you need to be peaceful.
Pay attention to the Good, so it grows.
Let go easily of what you do not want.
Forgive yourself for letting anything hurt you.
When another is upset, forgive.
Choose to be a calming influence while they release.
If needed, remove yourself so you can stay peaceful.
When in doubt, choose the Highest thought.
No sacrifice, always make sacred.
First Peace, then comes understanding.
Respect for Self creates respect for others.
Thoughts create your experience.
Choose to be happy and at peace.

Love Creates.
Love Enjoys.
Love Appreciates.

Healing

Relationships Heal

The purpose of relationships is to heal.

Relationships return to holiness what appears to be unholy.
Relationships return to wholeness what feels broken. Relationships remember God and Good in every creation.
Relationships see beneath the apparency to the essential gift of Love within.

What are we healing?
Heal judgments and comparison.
Heal fear and anger.
Heal the past pain and suffering.
Heal lack and littleness.
Heal guilt and self-doubt.
Heal unkindness and defensiveness.
Heal whatever is not whole and not loving.

How do we heal?
Give Love where there is a lack of Love.
Offer forgiveness where there is guilt and blame.
Be, do and give what appears to be needed.
Our Highest Purpose is to remember to Love and return to Wholeness and Holiness.

What Is Healing?

Healing is what we are here for together.

Healing is remembering Who You Really Are.
Healing is finding Inner Peace.
Healing is being happy.
Healing is listening within.
Healing is forgiving the world we see.
Healing is perfect trust in the True Reality.
Healing is knowing Love is my natural State.

We are here to heal and be healed.
We are here to extend Love to everyone.
We are here to offer Peace.
We can forgive all that is not Love.
We can see the Truth within each Being.
We can remember all of us are loved equally by God.

Let us remember and remind one another.

Levels of Healing

Some healing relationships are brief encounters or 'chance meetings', where our smile, our forgiveness of an error, or our Presence awakens in the other and in the Self a return to Love and Wholeness.

Some relationships are temporary agreements, where we spend months or years teaching and learning with one another, as we heal our pasts and remember our Holiness with forgiveness.
These relationships usually end after a time, when the current state of teaching and learning is complete.
While relationships change form, Love never ends.
Even when not together physically, the loving relationship is part of us forever.

Some healing relationships are long term agreements, where two people meet and make a commitment to teach and learn together for this lifetime.
Their work together may have bumps and 'scritches', but their commitment to do the work and remember Love endures.
They may struggle and have challenges, but their willingness to teach and learn, forgive and be forgiven, endures because of their commitment to their inner work.

Trust in the healing power of all relationships.

Healing The Fear

Fear contracts.

Love expands.

Fear withholds.

Love shares.

Fear defends.

Love is open.

Fear judges.

Love appreciates.

Fear condemns.

Love forgives.

Fear separates.

Love joins.

Fear acts out.

Love responds.

Fear withdraws.

Love reaches out.

Fear shuts down.

Love opens up.

Fear argues.

Love listens.

Fear excludes.

Love includes.

Fear worries.

Love blesses.

Fear justifies.

Love trusts.

Fear is stingy.

Love is generous.

Fear is pushy.

Love is patient.

Fear can be cruel.

Love is kind.

Fear is suspicious.

Love trusts.

Fear demands.

Love guides.

Fear cowers.

Love is courageous.

Fear takes care of its own.

Love is helpful to all.

Fear distorts our thinking.

Love sees clearly.

Fear speaks of wrongs.

Love speaks of value.

We are called to forgive, heal and release fear.

Giving Your Presence

What to do when someone is in intense grief, terror, anger or pain?

Give your deepest and most profound love, compassion and peace. Find the place of Love in you. Go to the place where you trust "All is well".

Find your own Center, through meditation, prayer, walking, inner listening, movement. From your center, visualize that you are extending your peace, your comfort, your understanding, your acceptance, your humanity to the person in need. Do all of this work on the inner where all your thoughts, words and deeds are received. Be at peace and know all is well.

Whatever the other being needs, give, unless it does harm. Give listening.

Give touch.

Give alone time.

Give reassurance.

Give faith.

Give distraction.

Give unconditional Love.

We cannot take away the emotions, attachments or conditions of the other, but we can be peacefully present for the other in their time of need.

Listen and honor what you hear in your heart.

Everything given with a truly loving intention will be received as a gift of Love.

Thank you for caring enough to give your very best.

Honorable Closure

How do you end a relationship, marriage, job, or friendship?

How do you know you are really done?

People often walk away without really finishing the real work, and then re-create it in their next experience.

People don't know how to come to a truly peaceful place, where "good-bye" is really "God be with You." When we are complete, we are grateful and at peace.

Honorable closure acknowledges:
1. learning and growth received,
2. challenges and difficulties experienced,
3. appreciation of gifts and blessings,
4. forgiveness and amends made.

Acknowledge within your self and with the other person all you have learned and how you have grown and benefited from the experience. Honor and express the challenges and difficulties that occurred and were endured during the time together. Offer gratitude and appreciation to the other for the benefits you received. Share your forgiveness and/or make amends for those places of unconscious or conscious errors of omission or commission. Often neither party is aware of what went unexpressed until the two have an opportunity to talk together. This is very valuable when done with the conscious intention for a peaceful conclusion.

Honorable closure includes heart to heart communication so all parties can express their part. If one party loses and is in hurt neither person is at peace. When we complete a relationship, job, living situation with respect, we are free to choose again without being haunted by the past or unconsciously repeating the same patterns. To move on, to create anew, to be fully inspired, requires honorable closure. Begin now.

Saying good-bye can be done with love, respect and profound gratitude and inner peace.

Forgiveness Releases

Whenever I am judging another, I am helping them stay stuck. Judgment stops the flow of life.

Judgment sends a projection of how I see the other.

It labels and expects the same.

Judgment supports the belief they have of themselves. Judgment sends a message that what I think matters.

Judgment comes from my limited knowledge.

Judgment interferes with their personal freedom of choice. Judgment gets me stuck in my own narrow perspective. Judgment strengthens the behavior I am judging in me.

Forgiveness sets me free.

Forgiveness allows me to see things differently.

Forgiveness opens the way for me to move see more. Forgiveness brings possibilities to my mind.

Forgiveness gives acceptance and permission for change. Forgiveness helps me forgive myself and choose again. Forgiveness supports my being unconditionally loving. Forgiveness sees the beauty and the blessing.

Judgment identifies the other with the behavior I have judged.

I believe I am right and use my mind to prove what I believe.

Forgiveness is a release from my limited perception.

I open the way for the other to be new in each moment.

I clear my belief and allow the other to choose again.

When I am willing to see beyond what I have judged (the apparency or the illusion) I enlighten the relationship and allow the love of God to enter, to heal and transform what is.

When I forgive, I step back and let Love lead the way.

I choose to forgive all things, hope all things and enlighten all things with Love. Love never fails.

Hold No Grievances

Love holds no grievances.
When I hold grievances, I feel unsafe.
When I release all grievances, I am in Love.

All unhappiness is holding grievances.
Where I feel most unsafe is where I have most grievances.
Where I judge, I am afraid.

I forgive all my grievances.
My Holiness blesses what my fear has judged.
My Holy Self blesses where my fearful self judged.
Only grievances hide the light in me.

I release all fear thoughts.
I bless my world.
I would see my whole and Holy Self by laying all grievances aside and remembering Perfect Love.

How are we to proceed?
Forgive all things today and everyday.
Lay all grievances aside now and always.
Awaken to the Love and Peace that abides in You.
To judge any of God's creations lays judgment on yourself.
What you judge you fear.
What you fear hides the light in you.
Your function is to shine your light.
Your function is to forgive.
Your function is to awaken your Holiness.
As we lay all fear side, we awaken in Perfect Love.
As we lay all grievances aside, we remember Who We Are.

Undo What Is Not True

Where you hold toxic feelings, you make yourself sick.
Where you hide secrets, you cannot heal.
Where you avoid darkness, you cannot see the Light.
To avoid conflict and negativity is to pretend all is well.
Love is not whitewash.
Love sets us free to trust in the Light
Love sees beneath the worldly apparency of error and sin.
Forgiveness is a spiritual laxative.
It gently releases unhealthy memories, beliefs and judgments.

All things can be healed.
All errors can be forgiven.
All problems can be resolved.
All difficulties can be overcome.
Bring them all to Light and Love.
In Light and Love errors are forgiven.
Conflicts are resolved.
Difficulties are overcome.
Sorrow and regret are released.
In the light of forgiveness, we can see things rightly.
We can see the gift in what is.
We can value the experiences we have chosen.
We can be responsible and responsive to whatever comes.

The Path of Light and Love is not for the Holy Pretender who hides behind kind words, but carries resentment and anger.

This Path is for those having the courage to speak their truth, forgive their mistakes and see things differently.

30 Days To Healing Relationships

Judgment leads to stuckness, repetition and replay of the mistake and victimization.

Unforgiveness generates pain, disease and inner conflict.

Lack of love begets fear, darkness and separation.

Letting go of the past fosters freedom and unlimited opportunities for choice.

Forgiveness promotes release, healing and inner peace.

Love creates miracles and natural joy and light.

30 Day Enlightenment Process

(Use this freely for healing and to see things differently.)

You may choose to continue it for a lifetime! It is miraculous.

1) Every morning, write 30 forgivenesses spontaneously, without thought or effort.

"I forgive......"

Then make the sound or tone " Ahh" for 2 or 3 minutes

(Aloud. if possible or silently, if in the presence of others.)

2) Then write 30 choices.

"I choose ....."

3) Before bedtime, write 30 gratitudes.

"I am thankful ....."

Sound or tone "Ommmm" for 2-3 minutes.

Forgiveness Is

Forgiveness is selective remembering—remembering what is good and beautiful and holy.

Forgiveness is selective perception--—seeing only wholeness and goodness beneath the apparency.

Forgiveness is selective vision—choosing what you want to behold and give your attention to.

Forgiveness is the only way to Love.

Forgiveness is recognizing and removing all obstacles to the awareness of Love's Presence.

Forgiveness is perceiving without judgment.

Forgiveness is cleaning your mirror.

Forgiveness is your only function as the Light of the World.

Forgiveness is letting Spirit interpret all things for you.

Forgiveness is trusting in God.

Forgiveness is seeing there is only Love and the call for Love.

Forgiveness is a gift to your Self.

Forgiveness is knowing your Brother is sinless.

Forgiveness is being willing to Love no matter what.

Forgiveness is letting go of what never was.

Forgiveness is seeing the world as a temporary learning laboratory.

Forgiveness is the key to happiness.

Forgiveness is letting go of what no longer serves you.

Forgiveness is letting Spirit guide you to heal all perceptions.

Forgiveness is an eraser filled with LOVE.

Let Go

To "let go" does not mean to stop caring.
> It means I can't do it for someone else.

To "let go" is not to cut myself off.
> It's the realization I can't control another.

To "let go" is not to enable.
> It is to allow learning from natural consequences.

To "let go" is to admit powerlessness.
> It means the outcome is not in my hands.

To "let go" is not to try to change or blame another.
> It's to make the most of myself.

To "let go" is not to care for.
> It is to care about.

To "let go" is not to fix.
> It is to be supportive.

To "let go" is not to judge.
> It is to allow another to be a human being.

To "let go" is not to be busy arranging all the outcomes.
> It is allowing others to affect their own destiny.

To "let go" is not to be protective.
> It is to permit another to face reality.

To "let go" is not to deny.
> It is to accept.

To "let go" is not to nag, scold or argue.
> It is to correct my own shortcomings.

To "let go" is not to criticize and regulate anybody.
> It is to become what I dream I can be.

To "let go" is not to regret the past.
> It is to grow and enjoy the present.

To "let go" is to fear less, and love more.

Thank God for the grace and willingness to Let Go!

Sacrifice

Are you giving all with no return?
Are you loving until you have nothing left?
Are you denying yourself while you care for others?
Do you feel invisible, overlooked, devalued?

Light attracts darkness to be enlightened.
Love attracts fear to be forgiven.
Healers attract the wounded to be healed.
Givers attract takers to receive.
Mothers attract children to cared for.
Saviors attract victims to be saved.

In this world of duality, we experience opposites.
When we choose to be one end of the polarity, we will attract the other.
People act more from their fear and guilt than from their Essence and inner calling.
To be given to, we must appear needy.
To be cared for, we must appear dependent.
To be saved, we must appear victimized.
To be forgiven, we must act guilty and fearful.
To be fed, we must appear hungry.

I prefer to be the Whole.
I prefer to be healer, giver, mother and savior.
I prefer to let Source lead me and direct me.
I prefer to give knowing I give but to myself and to the One.

Ways To Choose Again

There are two ways to let go and choose again.
One is to judge, destroy and get rid of what was.
This is painful and harmful to those involved.

The other is to create what one desires.
This way focuses on the future, on creating and building.
This way is grateful for the past which created the foundation for building something new.

Whether in dissolution of marriage, career or lifestyle, moving on into a new future can be gentle respectful and appreciative. As we are moving into a new era of consciousness, we need not judge, destroy or take vengeance on the past to choose a new tomorrow.

Vision	Imagine Your Ideal.
Faith	Trust you are supported.
Passion	Allow your Heart's desires.
Commitment	Never quit on your dreams.
Strategy	Listen within for the best way.
Action	Begin where you are and do it.
Gratitude	Appreciate every step.

New creations and new relationships are polluted by the past regrets and resentments.

Heal and clear what was to build a new tomorrow free of fear and filled with Love.

Holy Purpose

"The healing of the God's Son is all the world is for. That is the only purpose for it and therefore the only one it has."
(A Course in Miracles)

We are here for a Holy Purpose, to remember our Holiness. When anyone awakens to this truth, others are awakened.
We are Holy Loving Reminders to and for one another.
To seek for other rewards will yield disappointment, discouragement and hurt.

All relationships are for Holy and healing purposes.
To make our human relationships special is to ask for someone to give us what they often do not have. When we rely on an unreliable source, we can expect unreliable results.
One who judges cannot give total acceptance.
One who fears cannot give us reassurance.
One who is victim cannot be our hero.
One who is wounded cannot teach us our wholeness.
One who believes they are sinful cannot see our sinlessness.
One who sees darkness will not see our Light.

Usually we are to stay in constant communion with God, with the Spirit, with our Inner Teacher. On this Earth there are few beings who we consistently can count on to see us whole and Holy. We can rely on them to remind us of our Essence, the Light and Love for which we are created.

If you read these Relationship Reminders, it is highly likely that you are the most conscious and loving person you know.

Remember: Your mission is to be a Holy Loving and Peaceful Reminder for your Self and for others.

How Do I Make My Relationship Holy?

Our tendency is to make some relationships special.
We love and give to a few special ones more than to others.
We expect special ones to give to us in special ways.
We have reasons for loving some or caring for some or giving to some more than others.
When we listen within, we know there are no chance encounters.
Every relationship is for the purpose of healing
Every relationship is special.

To see All as sinless, to know All as Love itSelf, to behold the Light within each and every One, is to recognize and honor the Holiness, the Light and Love within ourselves.

Once we know this, we recognize our only function is to forgive (to erase with Love) everything unlike the Love we are.

To make every relationship Holy is to erase perceptions of unholiness.

This is a job for someone with patience, persistence, commitment, vision, faith, and the willingness to do the work!

Forgiveness is our function and our Holy Purpose.
Let us roll up our sleeves and do the job we came for.

The reward is our joy and inner peace, as we recognize the Holy and healing One we are.

Making a Real Difference

- Number of supporters makes no difference.
  Telling the High Truth does.
- Comfort makes no difference.
  Awareness does.
- Words make no difference.
  Living their meaning does.
- Money makes no difference.
  How you spend it does.
- Getting approval makes no difference.
  Positive regard and respect does.
- Accomplishing makes no difference.
  Happy intention does.
- Helping someone makes no difference.
  Seeing them whole and capable does.
- Showing up makes no difference.
  Paying attention and participating does.
- Being knowledgeable makes no difference.
  Sharing wisdom does.
- Making rules makes no difference.
  Living responsibly does.
- Working hard makes no difference.
  The cause you support does.

Remember, you make the difference!

Giving

Do You Serve or Take Care of Others?

Are you taking care of others?
Are you taking care of yourself?
Are you serving someone?
Are you serving yourself?
What is true service for yourself and others?

Forms of helpfulness and service have different foci and outcomes. We may learn to take care of our loved ones creating inappropriate dependency. If the other is truly unable to care for themselves in infancy or incapacitated, they are dependent.

Taking care of others who are learning to take care of themselves, creates false dependency or neediness to bolster the caregiver's self esteem or to create an obligation for reciprocity. Usually there is sacrifice and martyrdom in the one giving and guilt in the one receiving inappropriately.

Teach by example. Take impeccable care of yourself, your health and happiness. This teaches others to take care of themselves.

Serving others by believing their fears, needs, egoic fantasies will not support or serve. People rarely know what is best for them. Their learning is enhanced when they have the opportunity to experience the consequences of their own choices without interference or outside help.

True service is serving what is best for all.
When we follow inner guidance, serving what is best for all concerned, we trust we are giving from the heart, free from the need to be needed or to create approval, gratitude or indebtedness.

Helping

People we love have problems, get in trouble and behave in ways that are not highest and best for them (in our perception).

What are we to do?
Is there a way to be helpful without interfering?
Can we give advice?
Are we to share our experience?

If they seek help from us, we are to respond with Love, Wisdom and Discernment.

We are to listen to them.
We are to listen within.
We are to ask questions about their motivation, their goals, their choices, their beliefs.
We are to support them in thinking deeper and exploring their own experience so they can grow clearer in vision and stronger in discernment.
We are to share our experience only if invited.
We are to love and bless them.
We are to place them in Light of the Highest Outcome.

If you are not being asked for help, guidance, input, listening (possibly because they know you are judging their choices), then your input will be seen as interference and will be resisted, avoided, ignored or dismissed.

If not asked for help, don't try to advise.

Helping, Fixing, Serving

Service is not the same as helping.

Helping is based on inequality, it's not a relationship between equals. When you help, you use your own strength to help someone with less strength. It's a one up, one down relationship, and people feel this inequality. When we help, we may inadvertently take away more than we give, diminishing the person's sense of self-worth and self-esteem.

Now, when I help I am very aware of my own strength, but we don't serve with our strength, we serve **with ourselves**. We draw from all our experiences: our wounds serve, our limitations serve, even our darkness serves. The wholeness in us serves the wholeness in the other, and the wholeness in life. Helping incurs debt: when you help someone, they owe you. But service is mutual. When I help I have a feeling of satisfaction, but when I serve I have a feeling of gratitude. Serving is also different from fixing. We fix broken pipes, we don't fix people. When I set about fixing another person, it's because I see

> So, fundamentally, helping, fixing and serving are **ways of seeing life**. When you help, you see life as weak; when you fix, you see life as broken; and when you serve, you see life as whole.

them as broken. Fixing is a form of judgment that separates us from one another; it creates a distance.

When we serve in this way, we understand that this person's suffering is also my suffering, that their joy is also my joy and then the impulse to serve arises naturally - our natural wisdom and compassion presents itself quite simply. A server knows that they're being used and has the willingness to be used in the service of something greater.

We may help or fix many things in our lives, but when we serve, we are always in the service of wholeness.

--Rachel Remen, from *Zen Hospice*

How To Help

You can extend your love and blessings silently.
You can forgive yourself for being afraid for them.
You can give all problems to the Highest Good.
You can hold a vision of healing.
You can clear your own disaster pictures.
You can forgive your mistakes where you hold regrets.
You can learn to trust that everyone has their learning.
You can give it all to God.
You can talk to their guardian angel .
You can simply talk silently to that individual.
You can write a letter you need not send, because we are all receiving each other's messages telepathically.
You can Love them no matter what.
You can trust All Good and only Good.
You can know everything works together for Good.

Sometimes, when I feel regret about my past, I want to step in and shield someone else from similar mistakes.
This inter-fear-ence is simply a call for me to forgive myself, see how much I learned and choose to release myself and others to recognize that we learn the way we learn.

I forgive my mistakes and I forgive others.
I trust that with Love, all things are healed.
I know each one of us chooses our own life lessons.
To interfere (enter-fear) is not helpful.
To love and bless is my work.
I am willing.

Co-Dependence vs. Helpfulness

Co-dependents may care for others to raise their own self-esteem.
Do you feel powerful when you help another?
Do you seek appreciation?
Are you looking for reciprocity?
Are you attached to the results?
Are you seeking positive feedback?
Do you feel better about yourself?
Do you need to be needed?
Does it make you feel better to help?
Do you look for needy people?
Do you seek ways to be helpful?
Do you "know" what is needed?
You may be co-dependent.
You may benefit from having someone to take care of.
You may encourage people to be dependent on you.

Truly helpful people are guided to serve where it will be beneficial.
They facilitate people in being responsible, independent and helping themselves.

Do you help only when asked?
Do you respond when inner guided?
Do you only do as much as is needed?
Are you respectful of the other person?
Are you unattached to the outcome?
Are you conscious of seeing them whole?
Are you trusting your help is helpful?
Are you willing to give anonymously?

If so, you may be truly serving another, willing to give help only as needed. ***Do for others as you want them to do for you.***

True Service

To be in equal relationships, one must give equally.
To know equality, one must not compare or compete.
To know fulfillment, one must give all for the Joy of Giving.

Wherever we are withholding our gifts, talents and resources, we are cheating ourselves and our world. Wherever we are not sharing, speaking, and contributing our very best, we are denying our talents. We are the gift to be given. Where we diminish, deny or distrust the gifts we have within ourselves, we are being dishonest with ourselves and our community.

Whenever I have thoughts which are self critical, suspicious, resentful or guilty, I ask:
What have I withheld?
What am I not willing to give?
Where am I holding back?
What am I unwilling to say or do or give?
When I find that I am cheating a relationship of what I can give, I forgive my negligence. I choose again to live abundantly, to contribute fully and freely, to express my hopes and my dreams, to bring the gifts of my words and my activities to the table of life, where all may feast freely at the table of peace in love with one another.

Whatever I see needs to be done, it is mine to do!
Whatever I feel is missing, is mine to give.
Wherever I hear a need, it is mine to respond.
I need only listen within to those needs I feel calling me.
This is True Service.
Give All to All to Have All.
Life is for giving. You are the Gift!
Give and you will be enriched beyond measure.
This is your Treasure!

Can You Hear Me?

So often we listen only with our eyes and ears.
We judge the behavior, appearance and emotions of others.
We hear the words, the passion and the pain.
We fear the belligerence, the anger, and arrogant language.

Can we hear the cry for help?
Can we feel the lost soul seeking to be found?
Can we see the invisible yearning to be loved?
Can we forget the anger in their words?
Can we forgive the violent behavior?
Can we find a way to respect the being?
Can we erase our fear and respond to the need?
Can we love where love is forgotten?
Can we bring peace where peace is unknown?
Can we reach out when we may be resisted?
Can someone listen beneath the words?
Can someone see beyond the hurt?
Can someone hear the song of the heart?

No one is upset for the reason we think.

Can you be the one to care, to take the time, to put aside your defenses,
to trust in the request of every human to be heard and respected?

Listen with your heart and you will hear your heart song.

Taking Care of Others

It is futile and frustrating to try to fix, correct, or change others who have not asked for our help.

This is a form of judgment or attack on them and they will resist, resent, be offended or hurt.

They may withdraw, act out, blame you or feel defensive.

It is always best to help only when requested.

Being truly helpful requires:
- See the other person as whole and Holy.
- Give only what is being asked for.
- Give only if it is given with gratitude and love.
- There must be no sacrifice in the giving.
- Martyrdom causes guilt. Guilt perpetuates the pain.
- Listen within for the best Loving Reminder.
- Your Love and your listening are enough.
- If the other asks for advice or input, share.
- When in doubt, give what you would want to receive.
- Listen inside for your inner guidance.
- Respond always with respect and compassion.
- Never feel sorry or pity the other.
- Never get angry for your over-giving.

If you find yourself over-extended, forgive yourself and take care of yourself first.

A drowning person cannot be saved by someone who is drowning.

Giving To Wholeness

What is giving from and to Fullness and Abundance?

What is giving from and to Wholeness and Holiness?

I do not see my world nor the individuals in my world as needy, lacking or limited.

I see You and All as sometimes forgetting the Truth, denying your True Nature, losing sight of your Magnificence, your Prosperity and your Freedom.

I Am a Loving Reminder.

I awaken my world to remember what is always True beneath the physical illusion, the appearance of lack, littleness and limitation.

What I mean by the "appearance" is the world we make up of disease, poverty and fear based on our separation from our True Nature, from the Love We Are.

When we are healed, we realize Our Beauty, Goodness and Wholeness.

We experience Peace and "All is well."

Any upset, every fear or dis-ease is always a call for healing, for remembering, for forgiving, for releasing, for loving, for awakening, for connecting to God.

Giving from Fullness, Wholeness, Holiness and Abundance is realizing my True Nature.

I Am full, whole, holy and abundant.

I Am perfectly provided for in All that I have, All that I give and All that I Am.

When I am in the place of remembering I Am at peace and All is well.

Giving to fullness, wholeness, holiness, and abundance is realizing the Truth about those asking for help or calling for remembering and awakening.

No matter how Spirit calls me to respond, whether with money, advice, healing techniques, distraction, education, sharing, affirmation, affection, I am clear.

You are healed and whole.

You are prosperous and abundant.

You are unlimited and free.

You are beautiful and magnificent.

Giving a helping hand physically, emotionally, mentally or spiritually can be done with dignity and respect.

I give to you as I give to my Holy Self.

It must not be done with pity and sympathy, giving because I feel sorry for you and guilty about having it better than you do.

My relationship with those I serve comes as a Gift from my Spirit to yours.

My Holiness gives to your Holiness.

My Wellness honors your Wholeness.

My Fullness contributes to your Fullness.

My Good life celebrates your Abundant Life.

Excuse To Extend Love

"To Spirit, getting is meaningless and Giving is All." "To Have All, Give All to All. " (*from A Course in Miracles*)

On Valentine's Day, a day of celebrating love, it is appropriate to send love to those in your circle. Whenever we give Love, it is always received by the Spirit of the recipient. Whenever we give Love, it is always a gift to us.

My Valentine to God:

I love and value the gift of Life.

I praise you for giving me so many rich relationships and opportunities to remember Love.

May my life be a gift of love and appreciation to you.

My Valentine to my parents:

I love and value the gift of your lives. I appreciate you for giving me so much freedom and trust to live my life to the fullest. May my life be a gift of love and gratitude to you.

My Valentine to my children and family:

I love you and delight in the gift of your lives. You have blessed me with joy, as I have watched you enjoy all life has to offer. May you know always, I am loving and blessing you.

My Valentine to you, my friends:

I love you and totally enjoy our authentic loving relationship. You are a gift to me as you inspire, encourage and support me in sharing All I Am and All I Have for the Good of All. May my life continue to bless yours with inspiration, healing and peace.

My Valentine to mySelf:

Dear Betty Lue, I love you and appreciate who you are. Your loving, laughing, living and giving is a joy to me. I am always here for you, loving you and enjoying the beauty of your life.

Send your Love notes today, and you will receive all you need without every "getting" one.

Never Withhold Your Love

The only mistake we ever make is when we forget to love.

When we are limiting our Love and not giving our Best at all times, we feel guilty.

Our natural Self is Love and when we are not loving, we feel guilty and project our guilt onto the other with blame or avoidance.

Our guilt is about not freely giving our very Essence at all times. The guilt is camouflaged with an inner denial and projection onto the object of our guilt.

In other words, we make them responsible for our lack of love.

In all circumstances where we feel blame, the antidote is to give Love, give trust, give freedom.

When others feel unworthy, they resist and avoid love and teach those around them to stop loving.

Love them anyway.

Where there is lack, give more obviously.

Where there is fear, love more consistently.

Where there is guilt, forgive more openly.

Love is our reason for being.

Love heals all.

Ask

Have you asked the significant people in your life how you can serve and support them better?

Taking inventory means we can choose more of what is valuable and let go of what no longer has value.
It is valuable to stop to take stock of your life.
What you have attracted, achieved and invested in in the past may not serve and support you today.
By asking ourselves and others what is working and what isn't working, we can consciously and decisively remove what no longer serves and supports ourselves and others.
By adding those things which might better serve and support ourselves and others, we can change our habits and level of awareness.
We can live and give more in integrity with what really makes a positive difference.
Change works together for good when we dedicate all change to benefit ourselves and others.

Ask everyone who is important to you:
How can I serve and support you better?
Immediately make those changes unless it might harm you or the other.
Respond with respect and watch your relationships grow and prosper.

Respect
&
Responsibility

Self-Esteem

Self-esteem is the single most powerful healing agent.
Learning to truly love, trust and respect oneself empowers and supports great personal healing, growth and contribution.

If you are lacking in any of these areas, devote some time to building your relationship with yourself.

Steps to take:
- Assess your current state of Self-esteem.
- Recognize and clear the past.
- Develop strategies for daily self support.
- Stop self criticism and scaring yourself.
- Be kind and patient with yourself.
- Praise and support yourself.
- Look in the mirror daily and love you.
- Take time to please you.

Find someone you admire who loves, trusts, respects and believes in themselves.
Let their example teach you.
Read books on building self esteem in children and give the same to yourself.

Create the relationship you really desire with yourself.

Respect and Dignity

Respect and Dignity,
What will it be?
You get what you give,
Eventually.

Everyone deserves respect.
Stop judging, blaming or ignoring.
Look beneath their behaviors.
Listen beneath the words of the story.
There is a call for healing, a cry for Love.

Respond always with Loving kindness.
No name-calling.
No threats or demands.
No grudges and vengeance.
No dismissing or belittling.

Everyone deserves our loving attention.

Treat all beings with dignity and respect

This is healing you.

This is healing our relationships.

This is healing our planet.

Are You Willing to Be Responsible?

"How can I be responsible?
I am a victim of the world I see.
They are doing it to me.
They are wrong."

The way I respond to every circumstance determines the outcome, my memories, my healing, my health and my life story.

When I give the Love I Am, when I forgive and judge no one and nothing, when I acknowledge the call for help, the missed communication, the fear being shared, I will listen within and respond with Love, with courage, forgiveness, and Truth.

Healing will occur.
Help will be given.
Wholeness will result.
And Holiness will be my experience.

I am responsible for my experience.
No one can do anything to me that I have not agreed to.
I determine how I experience life by my interpretation.
No one can do harm unless I agree that harm is done.

I prefer to take responsibility.
I prefer to forgive, to heal, to bless, to be free from fear.
I prefer to trust, let go, grow, affirm and be the Love I Am.

I am learning.

I have learned healing my mind is my business.

I have learned that each person involved has their own unconscious investment in the outcome.

I have learned that I am the conscious one, the one choosing.

I have learned everyone does what they believe is "right" for them.

I have learned that no one knows what I really want except me.

I have learned to stop making assumptions.

I have learned to take nothing personally.

I have learned that all things work together for good.

I have learned to let go and let God.

I have learned that my Love and Peace of Mind are more valuable than anything the world has to offer.

I have learned that life works when I do the Work.

I have learned that I can and do make a difference.

I have learned that Love is more powerful than anything.

I choose to respond to all things with Love!

Change Takes Practice

Change takes time and practice + clarity and communication!
What took years to make, cannot be changed overnight.
It only takes one of you to apologize to undo the upset.
When you fall down, don't sit there and cry and wait for help.

- Get up and try again.
- Learn from your errors.
- Express what you really want.
- Soothe yourself with kind words.
- Acknowledge that each of you is doing the best you know.

You are beginners...*This is a new way of learning.*
RESPECT = Look deeper at what is needed and wanted.
Forgive your own mistakes and choose again for a better way.
RESPONSIBILITY = Be willing to respond with love.
If you don't have love to give...it means you have not taken good care of yourself and you need to fill up with Love for your Self first. Apologize for your inability or unwillingness to respond immediately in a kind and respectful way.
COOPERATION = When you can work together as a team, all seeking a win for all, you will change your ways.
The one who is most conscious and able will step up and do or say what is needed to bring the family together again. Helping and humor work well. Apologies and hugs will break the ice.

1. *Communicate the changes before you make them.*
2. *Ask for others support.*
3. *Remind people of your loving intention.*
4. *Tell the truth about your own needs or fears or resistance.*
5. *Forgive yourself and others for their impatience and resistance.*

You all want the same thing.

- **Respect** for yourself and others and from others to you.
- **Responsibility** for your own life and others being responsible for theirs.
- **Cooperation** yielding peace and harmony in your family.

Who Is Responsible?

The one most able to respond with Love is responsible. When there is a problem in a relationship, a divorce, a broken friendship a family issue, a financial dilemma, a simple disagreement, it is for the most conscious person to respond.

To respond with Love, you must be conscious and willing.

To respond with Love, you must be forgiving and loving.

To respond with Love, you must be respectful and kind.

Everything either emanates from a loving thought and intention or is an appeal for love. When anyone behaves in an unkind or thoughtless way, they are projecting their inner relationship with Self. They are expressing their need for help and healing. They are calling for forgiveness and love.

To take on someone's pain or problem or unkindness is to ignore their appeal for Love. To be wounded by another's unkindness disables one's ability to be truly helpful. To be harmed by a thoughtless or unkind word or deed is to generate more guilt in the other and intensify the problem.

It is up to the most conscious person:

To deny any harm.

To forgive any hurt instantly.

To speak and act in a conscious way.

To listen within for the healing response.

To give what you would want to receive.

To teach by example.

To offer peace to the relationship.

To extend love where it is lacking.

Expect to always be the conscious one.

Respond always with remembering Love.

Return to your natural state of wholeness and Holiness.

Treat Everyone With Respect

To love is to treat everyone equally.
Treat everyone, as you want to be treated.
Speak to others, as you want to be spoken to.
Think of others, as you want to be thought of.
Treat everyone, guest or family member, employee or employer, stranger or friend, with the same high regard.
Talk to those with whom you live with the same courtesy, as you would an honored guest.
To respect is to treat with courtesy.
To treat with courtesy is to use "Please" and "Thank you".
Take the time to listen to others' requests.
Request time to talk, rather than interrupt others.
Make your own requests known in a respectful manner.
We may take for granted those we love, especially family members.
We may find ourselves unconsciously treating them as in our family of origin.
We see them as objects, rather than as sensitive and significant people.
People learn to behave and respond as we train them to respond to us.
Ignoring those with whom we live teaches them to ignore us.
Respecting them teaches them to respect themselves and to respect us.
Most relationships endure and grow, when treated respectfully.

Teaching Respect and Responsibility

How do we teach respect and responsibility?

Be totally respectful and responsible.

To be respectful is to see beneath the apparency, to "look again".
To treat another with respect is to treat them with dignity, to be forgiving of their ignorance and error.
To be respectful is to have no expectations, to give the other full permission to be themselves, to have different values, behaviors, perceptions and dreams than we have.

To be responsible is to be able to respond with loving kindness to whatever comes our way.
To be able to respond we must take impeccable care of ourselves so we are not at the effect of others' ignorance, arrogance, attachments or fear.
We must let go and heal our own areas of unconsciousness to be free to respond as we are guided from within without attachment for the outcome.

To create better relationships, we must see ourselves as teacher and student.
To teach is to be peaceful, patient, non-judgmental, persevering and modeling the behavior and principles we want to teach.
Being respectful and responsible to ourselves is being true to the principles we are teaching, and knowing the reward is in giving the best we know.

Demonstrate Respect

Where is our respect for God?
Where is our respect for the sacred?
Where is our respect for the environment?
Where is our respect for all life?
Where is our respect for our bodies?
Where is our respect for our minds?
Where is our respect for our elders?
Where is our respect for our families?
Where is our respect for our learning?
Where is our respect for the wise ones?
Where is our respect for the healers?
Where is our respect for the teachers?

How do you demonstrate respect for others?
Give them your full attention.
Give them your sincere appreciation.
Give them positive regard.
Pay for the services rendered.
Be on time for all appointments.
Keep your agreements.
Be quiet when others are speaking.
Offer common courtesy.
Be truly helpful.
How do you respect yourself?
Listen to your real needs.
Pay attention to your health.
Keep yourself happy and inspired.
Give yourself what is good for you.
Associate with those who you admire.
Live your inspired life purpose.
Give your best always.

Freedom of Choice

To be responsible for your relationships, ask "How you are responding to other's choices to be, do and have what they want.

When someone makes a choice, do you respect their right to decide what is best for them?

Is it not best for you to free them and trust in their choice?

Questions to ask yourself:

Do you always want or expect to get your way?

Do you believe you know what is best for others?

Do you need others to do what you want to prove their love?

Do you trust others can love you and still be free to do what they want?

Can you affirm their being free and doing what they want?

Affirmations:

I can say 'No' to others without losing their Love.

Others can say 'No' to me without losing my Love.

Freedom of choice is a natural part of growing up and becoming a mature being.

First we are dependent.

Then we must become independent.

Only then can we learn to be interdependent.

Love is freedom and trust.

Respect Is Learned and Earned

Trust and respect are learned.

Trust and respect are earned.

Begin by respecting yourself consistently.

Be willing to treat yourself with impeccable care, honest values and consistent action.

Respect grows from within and shows up in how we live.

We teach people how to respect us by our example.

If we are respectful and kind in all our interactions, people trust us to be what we claim to be.

When we are in relationship with those who have experienced disrespect and dishonesty, they will expect the same from new relationships. We must patiently teach them we are different.

To respect someone who does not respect themselves, may require endless patience and kindness, forgiveness and love.

To change requires a willingness to let go of patterns which were chosen as a way of self-protection and self-care.

To unlearn unhealthy lifetime patterns, is a big undertaking and requires self-forgiveness and self -respect.

As I learn respect, I earn respect.

As I respect myself, others respect me.

As I respect myself, I respect others.

Look Again

How am I to look again and see things differently?
To what do I respond, to be responsible?
With whom do I cooperate and join for Good?

I see myself and others differently.
I must see myself and others as gifts of God.
I must recognize the goodness and beauty in each one.
I must respect the Love of Good in me.
I must respect my inner voice and calling.

Then **I am able to respond with Love.**
I respond with honesty, patience and trust.
I serve unconditionally from my heart.
I respond to the highest calling.
I give with Love, not duty or sacrifice.

Cooperation is joining with and for the Good.
I join with those who serve unconditionally.
I participate where there is joy and peace.
I am at One with nature and all creation.
I live in integrity with my Holy Self.

I respect God in Me and Thee.

I respond with the Love I Am.

I cooperate with the Good in Thee.

Relationship Creed

I pledge to give all of my Being to Love.

In trust and freedom

I experience Love,

I express Love,

I am Love.

I pledge to respect all beings,

to honor all paths,

to reverence all creation as sacred.

I commit my Self to be the Love I am.

to share the abundance I receive,

to offer the Truth I know,

to bring the Joy I experience.

I pledge to always remember the Source

from which all things come;

to be grateful for the joy of being here,

to facilitate our spiritual family-community

in the co-creation of a New World,

the Real World,

Heaven on Earth.

Betty Lue

Relationship Mission

- *Give* Gratitude
- *Teach* Love
- *Learn* Patience
- *Live* with Trust
- *Know* All *is* Well

Betty Lue Lieber, Ph.D., MFT

Born August 16, 1942 in Lansing, Michigan
Living in Hidden Valley Lake, CA and Walnut Creek, CA
Spiritual partnership with husband Robert Waldon since 1985
Mother, Step Mom and Active Grandmother of eight.
Licensed Marriage and Family Therapist since 1977
Creative Solutions Coaching and Counseling
Relationships and Communications Specialist
Whole Life Health Education and Consultant
Director, Reunion Center in Pleasant Hill, CA
Loving Reminders emailed daily worldwide since 1999
Facilitator, Lake House/Hermitage, Hidden Valley Lake, CA
Co-Director Positive Living Center, Hidden Valley Lake, CA
Co-Minister for Unity Center for Inspired Living, Brentwood, CA
Founder/Director Reunion Ministries and Living Ministry
Ordained Interfaith Minister and Spiritual Teacher
Teacher/Student of **A Course in Miracles** since 1977
Certified Feng Shui Practitioner
Certified T'ai Chi Chih Teacher
Author: **Loving Reminders, Peaceful Reminders, Relationship Reminders, Healing Reminders, Family Reminders, Healthy Reminders, Forgiveness, Pocketbook of Affirmations**
Ph.D. In Theocentric Psychology
Masters in Clinical and School Psychology
BS in Developmental Psychology

Websites:

LovingReminders.org

CreativeSolutionsCoaching.org

ReunionMinistries.org

ReunionLakeHouse.org

BettyLue.org

ReunionCenter.org

InspiredLivingCenter.org

PositiveLivingCenter.org

Reunion Center for Counseling, Healing and Growth
3496 Buskirk Rd, #103, Pleasant Hill, CA 94523
Unity Center for Inspired Living,
50 Sand Creek Rd., #140, Brentwood, CA 94513
Reunion Lake House/Hermitage Retreat
17664 Greenridge Rd., Hidden Valley Lake, CA 95467
Positive Living Center
17568 Spruce Grove Ext, Hidden Valley Lake, CA 95467

Appointments and Information:

Call 800-919-2392
Email:BettyLue@ReunionMinistries.org
Skype username: bettyluelieber.
Mail: Reunion Ministries,
17664 Greenridge Rd, Hidden Valley Lake, CA 95467
Founded in 1977, non-profit Forum for Global Holistic Spirituality through education, inspiration and service.
Non-profit, tax exempt 501(c)3

Free Daily Loving Reminders

Receive by email—bettylue@LovingReminders.org
View archived reminders at *www.lovingreminders.org*

Retreats

Reunion Lake House and Hermitage are available for individuals, couples, families and small groups.
Facilitated small group retreats are held several times during the year.
See website www.ReunionLakeHouse.org for application and pictures.

What is Reunion?

Reunion is the space of freedom and trust, where Love is remembered and Wholeness and Goodness are realized. **Reunion** is the space in which each individual can find and follow their own unique Spiritual Path and Essential Life Purpose.

We allow Spirit and inner guidance to lead us home to the Abundance of Joy and Love and Peace found in perfect Trust with God, the Good in All that Is. The Real Work here is to undo all self-made obstacles to the Awareness of Love's Presence, to reclaim our natural inheritance, to be whole and happy and free.

Our single error is separation from our True Identity, with one solution, **ReUnion.** The process of **reunion** is forgiving and releasing whatever keeps us separate from our Selves and our Source.

"Life is for giving and we are the gifts. It is in fully giving that we recognize the unlimited and magnificent gift of Love we are. The only mistake we ever make is when we forget to Love. Every thought, word and deed is our living prayer. Therefore, it benefits us and all creation to live in love and give abundantly."
Betty Lue

Reunion:

Forum For Global Holistic Spirituality

Reunion offers freedom & trust in which to:
   1. *Reclaim our True Self.*
   2. *Actualize our full potential.*
   3. *Balance our relationship with all life.*
   4. *Live our vision of cooperation and co-creation.*

Reunion Ministries

Reunion is a spiritual gift for all of us who seek reconnection with ourselves, with one another and with God.

Reunion Ministries is a non-profit church without walls, organization without requirements, programs without evaluation and spirituality without dogma. Reunion programs offer a forum for all to explore our own beliefs, to heal our hearts and open to inspiration within our own lives. These precepts are the guidelines through which we grow together in Trust and Freedom, the essence of Love ItSelf.

Precepts of Reunion

We are all Spiritual Beings.
All life is inter-connected.
Love is our natural state and the unifying field of all creation.
To create what is good, beautiful & whole is our call.
Forgiveness and freedom from judgment and fear
offer healing and love.
All relationships bring us into conscious awareness
of our blocks to love and our healing needs.
We are here to learn & teach what we are learning.
We respect all Beings, honor all Paths.
We listen within and serve the Highest Good for All.

Love Heals

&

Makes all things new.

The only mistake we ever make

is when we forget to love.

Remember:

Love You.

Love God.

Love Everyone.